PRAISE FOR
SOCIAL SKILLS FOR KIDS

"This book is a treasure trove of interactive social skills activities that every parent or educator should have on their shelf. Keri has made it really easy to understand how to find those teachable moments and start supporting students immediately."

—**Brandy Thompson**, author of *Learn, Grow, Succeed!: A Kid's Growth Mindset Journal*

"Spending special time together and learning how to empathize are among the greatest gifts we can give our children. *Social Skills for Kids* helps accomplish *both* through practical, fun activities. I highly recommend the I Hear You! Empathy Skills to any fellow caregiver of young kids!"

—**Tana Amodeo**, certified positive discipline parent educator and founder of SuchaLittleWhile.com

"As an LCSW working in a school system, this book is a dream! It's so well organized and easy to use. I love all the extras added in explaining social skills at different ages. Having a book of this quality that I can just grab and go with is something I treasure!"

—**Rachel R. Duke**, licensed clinical social worker

Adams Media
An Imprint of Simon & Schuster, Inc.
100 Technology Center Drive
Stoughton, Massachusetts 02072

First Adams Media trade paperback edition
June 2021

ADAMS MEDIA and colophon are trademarks of
Simon & Schuster.

For information about special discounts for bulk
purchases, please contact Simon & Schuster
Special Sales at 1-866-506-1949 or business@
simonandschuster.com.

The Simon & Schuster Speakers Bureau can bring
authors to your live event. For more information
or to book an event contact the Simon & Schuster
Speakers Bureau at 1-866-248-3049 or visit our
website at www.simonspeakers.com.

Interior design by Sylvia McArdle

Manufactured in the United States of America

3   2023

Library of Congress Cataloging-in-Publication
Data
Names: Powers, Keri K., author.
Title: Social skills for kids / Keri K. Powers, MA
EdHD, MEd, NCC.
Description: First Adams Media trade paperback
edition. | Stoughton, Massachusetts: Adams
Media, 2021. | Includes index.
Identifiers: LCCN 2021000312 | ISBN
9781507215753 (pb) | ISBN 9781507215760
(ebook)
Subjects: LCSH: Social skills in children. |
Socialization.
Classification: LCC BF723.S62 P69 2021 | DDC
155.4/182--dc23
LC record available at https://lccn.loc
.gov/2021000312

ISBN 978-1-5072-1575-3
ISBN 978-1-5072-1576-0 (ebook)

Social Skills *for* KIDS

From Making Friends and Problem-Solving
to Self-Control and Communication,
150+ Activities to Help Your Child
Develop Essential Social Skills

Keri K. Powers, MA EdHD, MEd, NCC

Adams Media
New York   London   Toronto   Sydney   New Delhi

CONTENTS

JOIN THE FUN! ENGAGEMENT SKILLS 143

DRIVER'S SEAT! SELF-CONTROL SKILLS 153

KEEP YOUR COOL! EMOTION-REGULATION SKILLS 173

INTRODUCTION

Weekly playgroups...one-on-one playdates...talking to people of various ages... virtual communication: Young children are exposed to a wide variety of social situations both in school settings and at home, but they don't always have the experience or knowledge to understand how to handle them. Learning key social skills, like making eye contact, speaking at an appropriate volume, sensing and respecting others' feelings, listening carefully, and exhibiting self-control, can help them feel prepared and approach these situations with excitement and interest instead of fear and stress.

Teaching your young child social skills early on—at roughly ages 1–8—offers a wide range of important benefits. Many studies show that strong social skills help kids reduce stress levels, play and work cooperatively with peers, achieve greater academic success, and develop deeper relationships with those around them.

Just as you begin teaching your child how to count, recite the alphabet, and learn colors at home, you can also teach them social skills by playing fun games at home. *Social Skills for Kids* is a collection of more than 150 activities designed to teach kids the social skills they'll need in childhood and beyond, such as:

★ Communication
★ Active listening
★ Cooperation
★ Responsibility
★ Empathy
★ Engagement (joining and participating in groups)
★ Self-control
★ Emotion regulation
★ Problem-solving
★ Respect

Each activity includes a list of materials, most of which are things you probably already have on hand. You'll also find a quick summary of the activity, the number of participants needed, where you can complete the activity (inside, outside, or online), and a list of the skills kids will practice while participating in the activity. The step-by-step instructions on how to set up and complete the activity or play the game will help you get to the fun parts quickly! To make the most of the activities, dive into the reflection questions, which will prompt kids to think about their experience playing the games and determine how to use those skills in other situations in their lives.

These activities can be done in a short amount of time, at home within your family, with a group of friends on a playdate or in the neighborhood, or even at a distance with family and friends on a video chat. The activities teach kids through imaginative play, hands-on experience, watching others model relevant skills, and person-to-person interaction. Every child is different, so this range of techniques allows you to choose which are best for your child's personality and age as well as the situation at hand.

Practicing the social skills featured in this book will give your child the emotional intelligence to feel happy and confident at home, at the playground, in the community, at school, and beyond! Let's get started!

LAYING THE GROUNDWORK

In this part, we'll explore what social skills actually are and why they're so important for your child, both right now and in the future. You'll also learn roughly when certain skills begin to develop, change, and flourish in childhood, so you can try to gauge where your child might be on the developmental spectrum.

You'll find important steps for teaching, modeling, and building social skills; examples of how kids learn about social skills in a variety of familiar settings; as well as easy-to-follow guides for leading conversations around social skills and new situations with your kids.

CHAPTER 1

SOCIAL SKILLS 101

WHAT ARE SOCIAL SKILLS?

Social skills encompass a range of proficiencies that people need in order to get along with others, actively and positively contribute in social settings, and form and maintain relationships. These relationships could be with family members, friends, fellow team or club participants, classmates, teachers, community leaders, and even future work colleagues.

Social skills help kids assess an environment and then choose actions that fit that situation or social interaction. Since situations and social expectations change depending on the setting, it's important that kids learn a wide variety of behaviors, words, and actions. It's also important for them to be able to recognize that their words and actions impact those around them.

Communication, turn taking, cooperation, empathy, self-control, emotion regulation, problem-solving, conflict resolution, and other abilities fall under the umbrella of social skills. To successfully participate in social groups, kids need to learn to not only communicate their own thoughts and feelings but also recognize the thoughts and feelings of others through their words and nonverbal communication like body language and facial expressions. They'll also need to develop skills around cooperating with others, such as taking turns sharing ideas or using materials, or working together to solve problems, whether they be social problems, academic problems, or challenges in team sports!

THE BENEFITS OF STRONG SOCIAL SKILLS

Social skills will play a very important role in every area of your child's life as they continue to grow and develop. Cultivating strong social skills can lead to a whole host of positive outcomes for your child.

Less Stress and Loneliness

Social skills can help ward off stress and loneliness in children. When kids are able to form and maintain relationships, they're less likely to be lonely. Plus, kids feel less stressed if they have trusted companions they can go to for support when needed. Research tells us that stress and loneliness are linked to both poor mental and physical health outcomes, so building strong social skills can actually help support positive mental and physical well-being for kids.

Academic Success

Strong social skills are also linked to academic success. Kids who are able to communicate effectively, actively listen to others, engage in problem-solving, and self-regulate their emotions do better in school, when measured by grades. Cooperative learning activities that students often undertake in school aim to prepare kids with real-world learning opportunities that can promote academic success. In these situations, kids who are able to communicate their ideas to peers, listen without judgment to their peers' ideas, and then use this information to plan for an assignment or project do better than those who struggle to work effectively in a team.

Additionally, when they face roadblocks in a group academic setting, kids who can self-regulate by being aware of their own emotions and using effective and appropriate calming strategies can refocus more quickly, thus losing less academic time. Self-control, also called impulse control, is also linked to academic success, as kids who are able to demonstrate self-control miss less instruction and have better peer relationships than those who struggle with self-control in the classroom setting.

Career Success

While their careers might seem like a long way off, time flies...and before you know it, your child will be applying for a weekend job or entering the workforce. Strong social skills prepare kids to be strong team members, compassionate colleagues, and responsible employees. A study funded by the Robert Wood Johnson Foundation examined the social skills of more than seven hundred kindergarten students, then followed their outcomes in adulthood. The study showed that there may well be links from behaviors associated with strong social skills—like sharing, resolving conflicts, and cooperating—to long-term successes, such as attaining higher education, landing higher-paying jobs, and experiencing better mental health. That study also found that children with strong social skills at an early age (kindergarten and first grade) were more likely to have full-time jobs 20 years later. Why could this be the case? The development of early social skills might create opportunities for strong social connectedness and meaningful engagement in academic and social situations.

WHEN DO SOCIAL SKILLS DEVELOP?

Social skills are constantly developing, from birth and even into adulthood. We are constantly receiving information from our environment that shapes the way we act in certain situations or with certain people. We are also constantly getting information from people around us—through verbal or nonverbal communication—that lets us know how our actions or words impact those around us or could potentially impact them.

As your child grows, you can expect to see some of the following social skills develop. As with most aspects of child development, progress will vary from child to child. Some of these skills may show up earlier than expected and some may appear later. Typically, this isn't cause for alarm, but always reach out to your pediatrician if you have concerns about your child's interactions, behavior, or health.

0–6 Months

Social skills are already beginning to develop in infancy. Infants begin establishing eye contact (a nonverbal communication skill), smiling when familiar people approach, and laughing in response to playful antics.

6–12 Months

During the second half of the first year, babies continue to establish stronger eye contact and are more able to maintain this eye contact. They may also smile when socially approached by new faces in addition to familiar ones, mimic behaviors like clapping or pointing, reach for caregivers, and respond to the facial expressions of others.

1–2 Years

During the second year of life, toddlers begin to develop basic self-regulation skills like settling or calming down (sometimes called self-soothing). They may also begin to offer toys to others and engage in role-play like mimicking routines and actions. They also begin to communicate verbally with simple words or phrases.

2–3 Years

At this age, kids begin to imitate pretend play actions, like making food or cleaning the house. They also begin to share their own desires or feelings by asking for what they want and using assertive verbal communication. They may also engage in caregiving behaviors—such as playing with a doll—showing concern and awareness for the needs of others. At this age, they usually also begin playing alongside other children, though they may not actually be playing *with* the other children (called parallel play).

3–4 Years

Kids in this age bracket continue to play beside others but might now begin to play with peers or siblings. Kids are able to take turns at this age and play with a group of 2–3 peers. They may also treat dolls and stuffed animal as if they are alive and engage in social play with these items. At this age, kids could start talking about their feelings in a variety of situations. They might also demonstrate an awareness of family and social rules, especially when they know they have broken the rules! Kids may also show spontaneous kindness and care toward others.

4–5 Years

During the fifth year of life, kids are able to engage in turn taking and imaginative play with others. In their play, they may be working together toward a common goal, showing early cooperation skills. They begin to engage in imaginative play that expands outside of their own experiences, like pretending to be a barista at a coffee shop. Kids can also play games with simple rules, like hide-and-seek or freeze dance. At this age, kids are more communicative and engage in conversations with same-age peers.

5–6 Years

At this stage in life, kids may begin to engage in play with others with a shared goal. They may play together in an imaginative way, like pretending to be characters from their favorite TV show. Or they might be playing together in an imaginative mission, like defending townspeople from a fire-breathing dragon! They may also begin playing board games with adult guidance. Kids might also engage in negotiations during play, like, "You be the knight this time and I will be the dragon, and next time, I'll be the knight and you can be the dragon!" Kids at this age are usually able to engage in more thoughtful conversations with peers, as they begin to ask questions about other kids' interests, experiences, and ideas.

6–7 Years

Kids continue engaging in play with peers and may play with larger groups. They will also begin to make up their own games with their own rules in a group, which may require some negotiation. They also play cooperative games and are beginning to learn to cope with losing.

7–8 Years

Social and cognitive skills are really advancing now! Kids continue playing cooperatively with peers, creating their own games, and engaging in play that is outside their personal experience (like captaining a pirate ship). However, play at this age is often less imaginative and more goal directed or competitive. At this age, kids are better able to deal with losing competitive games and have an understanding of sportsmanship.

Kids are becoming very aware of other people's feelings and more aware of others' perceptions and intentions. They are also aware that multiple feelings can exist together. For example, they recognize that they can feel excited about the big game but also nervous about their own performance in the game. They demonstrate the ability to cognitively process things they are seeing in their environments and use this information to choose appropriate actions for themselves. They can plan their actions and think ahead. For example, when they want to invite a friend to play, they can plan an activity in advance. Kids at this age are more able to consider several aspects of a problem at once when they engage in problem-solving tasks.

Special Considerations That Can Impact Social Development

While development of social skills generally follows these age ranges, there will be variance among children, especially those with diagnoses that impact social interaction. For children diagnosed with autism spectrum disorder, engagement skills, communication skills, self-control, and other social skills may not follow the expected developmental pattern. Likewise, children diagnosed with attention deficit hyperactivity disorder may struggle to demonstrate age-expected self-control or emotion-regulation skills.

If your child has been diagnosed with a condition that impacts their social interactions and development or communication, talk with your pediatrician to learn more about expected development and strategies for helping your child make developmentally and individually appropriate progress. The activities in this book will still be fun for you and your child! Talk to your child's providers about which areas (e.g., communication, emotion regulation, etc.) would be best to focus on right now, and choose activities that target those skills.

HOW KIDS DEVELOP SOCIAL SKILLS

The main way that children learn social skills is by watching the people around them and then practicing those skills in their own lives. Kids pick up on social skills starting as early as birth! Let's think about some specific examples.

★ It's that late-afternoon time frame. It has been a while since lunch, and nap time is over. Dinner won't be ready for a while, but your child is hungry. Your child can observe how siblings ask for a snack when they're hungry and use this example as a means for obtaining his own snack. He sees a sibling say, "Mom, can I please have a banana?" and can then mimic the behavior to obtain a snack for himself. If he's a baby taking in all this information, he may not ask quite so directly. But he may make some sounds in an attempt to get what his sibling has just gotten. Observing members of the family gives babies and kids information about how to act or how to obtain the things they need in the home setting.

★ You're at the grocery store and there is a long line. Your 3-year-old child is sitting in the seat of the shopping cart and looks around at the others in the line. Waiting in a long line might be a new experience for your toddler, but seeing how people wait patiently in line at the grocery store gives her important social information about what is expected in this particular setting.

★ At the park, your child sees others playing a game that looks really fun. She does not know these children and seems unsure how to join the game. While she watches them play, she may see others join the game. Observing how other children join the game gives her information on how she can get in on the fun too.

Three basic steps make up the important task of navigating social situations like these: seeing, thinking, and acting.

Step 1: Seeing

Seeing involves noticing and taking in social cues, and it's critical for developing social skills because it is the process of observing and taking in important information about the environment and others in the environment. Seeing can take on many forms:

★ Children observe what adults are doing in the environment around them.

★ They can also pick up on the tone of the environment. Is it a playful, casual environment, or do others seem serious?

★ When kids face a new situation, they may also observe other kids' behaviors. What are the other children doing? How are they completing the task? How are they playing?

★ Kids can pick up on other people's reactions. They may notice that a friend seems excited to see them and then move to give the friend a hug. Or they may notice that a sibling seems bored with the game they are playing, which may lead them to suggest a new game.

Kids use this information to guide their own actions, which in turn directly impact others. If the seeing or observing does not take place, kids may choose actions or behaviors that do not fit the environment or situation.

Step 2: Thinking

The second task, thinking, involves interpreting the observed information by thinking about what has been observed and what one can do with the information. For example:

★ What does it mean when I see all the other kids sitting quietly on the carpet facing the teacher?
★ What does it mean when my friend is sitting alone with tears in her eyes?
★ What does it mean when my mom is on the phone in her office?

Thinking also involves interpreting the intentions of others, as in:

★ What did he mean by that?
★ What does her action tell me?

This is a skill that certainly develops over time, but it is an important piece of the social-skill-development puzzle. You can practice while out in the world. For example, at the playground, when your child jumps in front of a friend in line for the slide, they will likely get a strong negative response from their friend. The friend might yell, "Hey, she cut in line! It's not her turn! I was waiting." Over time, kids will internalize that social cue: *My friends feel upset when I don't wait patiently and give them their turn.* Others will benefit from some adult guidance here. "Notice how your friend's face is showing a frown and her arms are crossed. How do you think she's feeling? Why do you think she might feel that way? What is a different choice you could make to help your friend feel better?"

Step 3: Acting

Once information has been observed and thoughtfully considered, kids can act in a way that fits the context (or doesn't!). While younger kids sometimes jump right to acting, following all three steps of the process will ensure a better outcome.

Children as young as 3–5 can begin to think ahead and plan their actions by anticipating future consequences, such as moving closer to the bottom of the staircase before jumping off the final step, because they anticipate a painful physical consequence if they jump off the top step! Though younger kids can certainly observe and learn from social consequences (like, *My sister cries when I pull her hair. I don't want my sister to be sad, so I won't pull her hair anymore*), researchers believe age 7 is the developmental age at which most kids are better able to develop rational thinking, have an internalized conscience, and control their impulses in social settings (sometimes referred to as the "age of reason"). In this phase, they are more aware of not only how others are feeling but also how their behaviors can impact those emotions. They can use the information they have observed, think it over rationally, and then choose appropriate actions. While there are certainly individual differences, prior to this age, many children still view themselves as the center of their own world and have difficulty seeing things from someone else's perspective.

Building Social Skills Through Spoken Observations

As kids get older, around 5–8, they're more developmentally able to take in direct instruction and receive feedback or suggestions on these skills through thoughtful questioning with trusted adults. This can be as simple as overhearing a parent wonder aloud about a situation. Spoken observations can help kids better understand what it looks like to follow the three steps: observe others (seeing), think about the needs and the expectations of the social situation (thinking), and then choose an action that fits the situation (acting). Let's look at some specific examples:

⋆ You have just boarded a subway car and sat down with your child. You anticipate that your child might use a louder voice than is appropriate in this setting, so you say, "Hmm, I noticed when we got on this train car that everyone is sitting quietly. Some people are reading, and others are listening to music. I think the other passengers might be bothered if I have a loud phone conversation with my sister right now. I'll send her a text message now and call her later when we get home."

⋆ You and your child have arrived at story time at the local public library. The activity today is a book reading followed by a craft at a table with peers. This is your child's first experience with an activity like this, so you say, "I noticed when we walked in that all the other children are sitting on the carpet with their grownups. They have their hands in their laps and are looking toward the librarian. Let's join them and do what they are doing!" After the story, when you move to the craft table, you say, "Look at all these cool supplies! I see there are several other children at the table too. It looks like the supplies are for everyone to use. Let's choose just a couple of these and a couple of those so that there are enough supplies for everyone."

⋆ You arrive at a birthday party with your child. The other children are clearly excited, running around the space, yelling after one another and playing games. You expect that your child might become a little overexcited if he joins in with the running group, so you say, "Wow, birthday parties are so exciting! It seems like everyone is having fun. I'm noticing that Jaden's grandmother is covering her ears. All that running and yelling might be hurting her ears. Look, Jaden's mom set up a fun game over there, and your friend Max is playing. Why don't we join him?"

Recognizing others' feelings and how our own actions may impact them is a critical component of social-skill development, and hearing you observe these will help your child begin thinking about these processes. Over time, they'll grow to internalize this process for themselves.

HOW TO PROVIDE GENTLE GUIDANCE FOR SKILL DEVELOPMENT

Sometimes, when you find yourself in a situation in which your child needs guidance in solving a problem, it can be hard to find the right words or the right roadmap. As you guide your child through real-time problem-solving in social scenarios, you can think of the IDEAL method suggested by the American Psychological Association to guide your conversation:

* Identify the problem and the feelings involved in the situation.
* Determine possible appropriate solutions.
* Evaluate each possible solution.
* Act, after choosing the best solution.
* Learn from the situation so you can apply this information later!

Here's what that might look like:

Situation: Your 7-year-old child comes home from soccer practice complaining that Jamie would not pass the ball to him. "Jamie is such a ball hog! I was open, and I told him that I was open, but he still wouldn't pass to me. I don't even want to play on the team anymore!"

Identify the problem and feelings:

Adult: "Wow, it sounds like soccer practice was really hard today. You're feeling frustrated."

Child: "Yes, and mad! It's not fun to play when someone hogs the ball."

Adult: "It sounds like you're not enjoying playing your favorite sport right now because of what happened today with Jamie."

Child: "Yeah, it's not fun when people don't share the ball."

In this situation, the feelings have been labeled (frustrated and mad), and the problem has been identified: A previously enjoyed activity isn't feeling fun right now because of a peer interaction.

Determine possible solutions:

Adult: "What do you think you should do about this problem?"

Child: "I just want to quit the team. It's not fun anymore!"

Adult: "Hmm, that's one idea. Let's see if we can think of some others."

Child: "Well, I guess I could talk to him and ask him to pass the ball."

Adult: "You could definitely do that. He might not know how you feel."

Child: "Or I could tell everyone else on the team not to pass the ball to him."

Adult: "That's another idea. I wonder if we could think of something else."

Child: "Maybe I could ask Coach Tre if he could remind everyone to pass the ball when people are open and have a good shot at the goal."

Adult: "That's another great idea. Let's think about what might happen if you tried each of these solutions."

Evaluate solutions:

Solution 1: *Adult*: "If you decided to just quit the team, you would probably really miss playing soccer. It's your favorite sport! Let's see if another solution might be better."

Solution 2: *Adult*: "You could talk to Jamie and tell him how you feel. You could tell him that you feel frustrated when he won't pass the ball to you and ask him to pass the ball when you're open near the goal. He might not know how you feel, but if you share how you're feeling, he might be more willing to pass the ball."

Solution 3: *Adult*: "You could tell everyone else not to pass the ball to Jamie. But that doesn't really seem like good sportsmanship, right? That might cause a big problem between teammates."

Solution 4: *Adult*: "You could talk to your coach about the problem. He could spend some time at practice reminding everyone to work together and be teammates. He might even have everyone practice some passing drills to make sure everyone knows how to do it. Which solution do you think would be the best one?"

Child: "Well, I'm not sure I'm comfortable talking to Jamie about how I feel about it. So I think I'll just talk to Coach Tre first instead. That seems like the best to me."

Adult: "I think that's a great solution. Coach Tre will be able to help."

(continued on next page)

Act with the chosen solution:

At soccer practice, your child can arrive early to speak with the coach about the problem.

Child: "Coach Tre, can I talk to you?"

Coach: "Of course. What's up?"

Child: "Last week at practice, I was really frustrated because Jamie wouldn't pass me the ball. I kept telling him I was open, but he just kept the ball. I was just really upset and was wondering if we could maybe talk about passing or practice passing at practice."

Coach: "Thanks for letting me know how you felt about that. We can definitely talk about passing. It's always important to practice!"

Learn from the situation:

Adult: "I'm so proud of you for picking a helpful solution to this problem from soccer. What do you think you learned from this?"

Child: "Adults really do want to help. Coach Tre knew exactly what to do, and practicing passing at practice really did help everyone on the team. And I'm glad I didn't quit just because I was mad. I would have really missed soccer!"

Adult: "That's great! It's always okay to talk through problems and ask for help. And it's important not to make big decisions or act when we're angry. Taking time to talk through the problem helped you make a calm decision."

Guiding kids through this process of thinking about the problem and the feelings involved and then considering possible solutions can help them evaluate different aspects of the problem and think about others who are involved. Ruling out solutions that may have negative outcomes is also important, as you are encouraging kids to look ahead and make predictions about what might happen if they take certain actions. It can also encourage them to pause and take time to think over the problem before they act, an important impulse-control skill in all areas of life.

GENERAL TIPS FOR HELPING KIDS

We've already discussed many ways you can help your child "in the moment" when they are encountering social situations. The following are additional ways to provide safe spaces for your child to learn social skills:

★ Give them lots of opportunities for practice! Join regular play groups, be around neighbors, and visit the park.

★ Play games together so they can learn about turn taking and winning and losing graciously.

* Hold casual playdates so they can practice sharing and doing what someone else chooses.
* Video chat with friends or family members so they can practice active listening and picking up on nonverbal cues in an electronic setting.
* Teach your kids how to identify and name their own feelings and practice noticing feelings in others.
* Teach empathy. Look for opportunities to talk about how others might be feeling. Model for kids how to imagine how someone else might be feeling.
* Role-play before situations so kids can practice ahead of time. For example, before heading to the park, role-play how to ask to join a game. Before going to art camp, role-play complimenting a peer's work.
* Give your child lots of opportunities for independent success—only step in when necessary.
* Offer your child gentle, encouraging feedback about social skills.

Giving children lots of varied opportunities for learning while offering constructive, compassionate feedback and gentle guidance will help them develop the important social skills they need for success in school, on the playground, and beyond.

2

ACTIVITIES

In this part, you'll find more than 150 activities that you can do at home, in the neighborhood, in your community, or on a video chat with friends and family to practice these important skills. Each activity includes a suggested age range, a list of helpful materials, skills that the activity focuses on, step-by-step instructions, and any necessary teaching or preparation tasks to complete before the activity. You'll also find discussion questions for after the activity to get kids thinking about how they can transfer their learning to real-life scenarios. These discussion questions are an important transition to help kids process what they've just done and consider how it relates to the world around them. You'll find specific questions tailored to each exercise, but you can always ask additional open-ended questions, like, "What was fun/difficult/easy about this activity?"

Keep in mind that the age ranges given are simply suggestions and that kids develop at different rates (and that's okay!). Pick and choose activities that you think will work best for your child. And if an activity doesn't go how you hoped it would the first time, give it another try later.

On the other hand, if your child really enjoys any particular activity, feel free to repeat it over and over. Kids love to feel a sense of mastery when they are able to accomplish a task or challenge. Make small changes to keep things interesting or make it your own by tailoring an activity to your family's interests to really get buy-in from your child.

Most importantly, *have fun together*!

CHAPTER 2

LET'S CHAT! COMMUNICATION SKILLS

WHAT IS COMMUNICATION?

"Communication" refers to the ways that we share and relay ideas. Communication can be both verbal and nonverbal. Verbal communication refers to the way we actually talk to one another. This can include spoken words, written or typed words, the tone of voice we use, and even the volume of our voices. After all, it's not just what we say but *how* we say it that communicates an important social message!

Nonverbal communication refers to the way we communicate with our movements, postures, facial expressions, and bodies. It can include things like nodding, making eye contact, turning our bodies toward those who are speaking, smiling while others talk to us, and more. We can activate kids' understanding of this nonverbal communication by demonstrating postures and asking them to think about how they would feel if someone stood or looked like this when they were speaking. Here's an example: "How would you feel if you were telling me a story about something really exciting that happened, and I was frowning with my arms crossed and looking at things around the room? But how would you feel if I was making eye contact, nodding, and looking excited while you were talking to me?"

WHAT DOES COMMUNICATION LOOK AND SOUND LIKE?

Communication can sound like a verbal conversation, but it's so much more than just speaking. It can look like a frown, slumped shoulders, or excited jumps and smiles. It can also look like a written note or text message. Some examples of communication that kids engage in include:

★ Talking to family members and friends
★ Drawing a picture for a friend to cheer them up
★ Crying or frowning after a peer takes a toy without asking

COMMUNICATION IN KID-FRIENDLY TERMS

To explain communication to your kids, try saying something like this:

We all have things we want to say and ideas we want to share. There are so many ways that we can do this. We can tell someone what we are thinking with our words. We can show someone how we are feeling with our faces. We can draw a picture that shows how we are feeling too. All these things are communication. Communication means that we share our ideas, thoughts, or feelings with our words, bodies, faces, writing, or drawing.

WHY COMMUNICATION SKILLS ARE IMPORTANT

Communicating effectively is a huge piece of the social-skills puzzle! Infants use cries to communicate their needs to caregivers. Toddlers use their behavior to communicate their wants and needs. Children use their words, faces, behaviors, and more to share their ideas and experiences. Communication skills are how we share our thoughts, our needs, our dreams, our ideas, and so much more. Being able to communicate effectively with others promotes group cohesion, group effectiveness, and feelings of connectedness.

WHERE AND WHEN KIDS WILL USE COMMUNICATION SKILLS

Communication is everywhere! Kids will communicate their needs, fears, and wants at home. They'll communicate their creativity and imagination in play settings. They'll communicate their ideas and questions in the classroom. Providing them the skills to communicate effectively with words and actions will give kids a leg up in all settings, as they'll have the confidence to speak up and ask for what they need and share their own unique ideas.

LOOKING AHEAD

In this chapter, you'll find games and activities to help your child practice these verbal and nonverbal communication skills. Give them a try as a family or play with friends in the neighborhood. Some of these activities can even be played with grandparents, cousins, or friends on a video chat.

BABY TALK

Babies actually have lots of ways of communicating, even though they may not be able to verbally share what they want to say. While they might not understand your responses right now, your verbal responses will encourage communication and give babies a sense of accomplishment when their attempts at communication are rewarded.

Age Range:	1–2
Skills:	Nonverbal cues, body language
Materials:	None
Number of Participants:	Baby and caregiver
Where to Play:	Inside or outside

HOW TO PLAY

★ When your baby makes attempts at communication using cries, arm waves, or nuzzles, respond verbally to them.

★ For example, when your baby nuzzles in close to your arm, say, "It looks like you're hungry! Let's get you some milk. Thanks for telling me what you need!" Or when your baby reaches out to touch the book you're reading, say, "Oh, you are interested in the story! Let's turn the page and see what happens next."

THINKING BACK AND LOOKING AHEAD (FOR CAREGIVERS)

★ How did my baby communicate with me today?

★ In what other ways can I respond to my baby's attempts at communication?

CHITCHAT

While they may not be able to verbally respond to what we say, babies get a lot out of a real conversation with a caregiver. Spend time carrying on a "conversation" with your baby, even if it feels a little one-sided. Simulating regular conversations like this while offering pauses for your baby to interject will help them build conversation skills before they're even talking! They'll learn about the give and take in a conversation and enjoy being a part of the chitchat.

Age Range:	1–2
Skills:	Nonverbal cues, body language
Materials:	None
Number of Participants:	Baby and caregiver
Where to Play:	Inside or outside

HOW TO PLAY

★ At a special time each day, like after bath time or during a diaper change, make time for a conversation with your baby.

★ Maintain eye contact with your baby and engage in physical touch by holding hands or helping your baby sit up in your lap if developmentally appropriate.

★ Talk to your baby like you would an older child. Simply share about your day or ask them questions about their day. After asking them questions, pause, make eye contact, and give them a chance to "respond." They may respond with coos, simple eye contact, or playful kicks.

THINKING BACK AND LOOKING AHEAD (FOR CAREGIVERS)

★ How did my baby communicate with me today?

★ In what other ways can I respond to my baby's attempts at communication?

BOOK TALK

Engage your baby in conversations about the books that you read, even if they can't verbally respond just yet. Asking them questions and pointing out exciting things on the pages will help your baby build vocabulary and grow their confidence for trying to communicate.

Age Range:	1–2
Skills:	Nonverbal cues, body language
Materials:	Books
Number of Participants:	Baby and caregiver
Where to Play:	Inside

HOW TO PLAY

★ During book time, engage your baby in conversations about the story. Say things like, "Wow, I wasn't expecting him to do that. Did you know that was going to happen?" Pause and give your baby a chance to respond!

★ Point out exciting or important details on the page. "Do you see this blue dog? That blue dog looks fuzzy and soft. Would you like to play with a blue dog?" Again, after each question, pause, make eye contact, and give your baby a chance to respond.

★ When your baby responds with small sounds or kicks, or reaches for the page, respond as if they have spoken to you. "Oh, really?! You did see that coming? Wow, you're really perceptive." Or, "You think a blue dog would be fun? I think so too."

THINKING BACK AND LOOKING AHEAD (FOR CAREGIVERS)

★ How did my baby communicate with me today while I read them this story?

★ In what other ways can I respond to my baby's attempts at communication?

VOLUME HOPSCOTCH

Being aware of one's own voice volume is important for all kinds of social interactions. This activity will help kids develop an understanding of voice levels using a scale and physical body movements. Help them think about when each voice level on the scale is appropriate to use.

Age Range:	3+
Skills:	Communication, voice levels
Materials:	Chalk
Number of Participants:	1+
Where to Play:	Outside

BEFORE YOU START
★ Draw a straight hopscotch course numbered 0–10.
★ Talk about the numbers and how they relate to voice levels. Zero is a silent voice and ten is the loudest voice ever. Five is a normal speaking voice. Demonstrate each of these.

HOW TO PLAY
★ Players will stand at the start of the hopscotch course.
★ You will ask, "How's my voice volume?" in different voice levels.
★ Players will hopscotch to the number that they think best represents your voice volume.
★ Players can explain their number choices before returning to the start.
★ Continue asking, "How's my voice volume?" in different voice levels, letting players hop to the number that best represents the voice level.

THINKING BACK AND LOOKING AHEAD
★ When is a zero voice level good to use?
★ When is a ten voice level good to use?
★ In what kinds of situations or places should we not use a ten voice level?
★ How do you think you can help yourself remember what kind of voice level to use?

I FEEL, I NEED

Sharing personal needs is an important social skill for all kids. When big feelings sneak in, saying or asking for what they need will help kids regulate their emotions appropriately. This activity will help kids consider their own needs and practice asking for things assertively.

Age Range:	3+
Skills:	Assertiveness
Materials:	Scenario cards (optional—you can also simply state scenarios), a feelings chart or cards with emojis
Number of Participants:	1+
Where to Play:	Inside or outside

BEFORE YOU START

★ Talk about things we might need when we have big feelings. When we are angry, we might need time alone. When we are sad, we might need a hug. Make a list together of things the children participating might need when they have strong emotions.

HOW TO PLAY

★ Read one of the following scenarios to the participants:
  • Imagine that someone knocked over the tower you were building.
  • Imagine that you lost your favorite stuffed animal.
  • Imagine that you fell down while riding your scooter.
  • Imagine that someone laughed at your artwork.
  • Imagine that you aren't feeling very well.
★ Participants will then use the feelings chart or emoji cards to identify how they would feel in that specific situation, by saying, "I feel…"
★ Then, participants will think about what they might need in that situation. They will share by saying, "I need…"

THINKING BACK AND LOOKING AHEAD

★ What was hard about this activity?
★ What was easy about this activity?
★ Why do you think it's important to tell people how you're feeling?
★ Is it okay to ask people for what you need? How do you think asking for what you need can help when you have big feelings?

To help kids learn about big feelings, spend some time reading books together about coping skills or calming strategies. *Cool Down and Work Through Anger* by Cheri Meiners is a great place to start with some practical, age-appropriate calming strategies kids can use.

CAN YOU HEAR ME NOW?

Using an appropriate voice level is an important skill for kids to develop for school, community groups, or just play. This activity will help kids visually see how physical distance from others should impact the level of their own voices.

Age Range:	3+
Skills:	Communication, voice levels
Materials:	None
Number of Participants:	2+ (even numbers)
Where to Play:	Inside or outside

BEFORE YOU START

★ Talk about different voice levels. Demonstrate for the participants what a whisper, normal speaking voice, and loud speaking voice sound like.

★ Let players practice before they start.

HOW TO PLAY

★ Players will stand across from each other.

★ One player will whisper, "Can you hear me now?"

★ If the other player can hear them, they will say, "I can hear you," and take one step backward.

★ Repeat this until the player who is stepping backward can no longer hear the other player.

★ Then, the first player will raise their voice to a normal speaking voice and ask, "Can you hear me now?"

★ If the other player can hear them, they will say, "I can hear you," and take one step backward.

★ Repeat this until the player who is stepping backward can no longer hear the other player.

★ Then, the first player will raise their voice to a louder speaking voice and ask, "Can you hear me now?"

★ If the other player can hear them, they will say, "I can hear you," and take one step backward.

* Repeat this until the player who is stepping backward can no longer hear the other player.
* Restart in the original position and switch roles.

THINKING BACK AND LOOKING AHEAD
* What did you notice about the distance between you with whispering voices?
* What did you notice about the distance between you with normal speaking voices?
* What did you notice about the distance between you with louder speaking voices?
* What is it like when someone is very close to you but uses a louder speaking voice?
* When do you think it might be a good time to use a whisper voice?
* When do you think it might be a good time to use a normal speaking voice?
* When do you think it might be a good time to use a louder speaking voice?

SECRET OBJECT

Descriptive communication and active listening are important components of everyday conversations. By using descriptive communication, kids are better able to express their own ideas to others in ways that truly convey what they want to say. And active listening shows others we care while also helping us get all the information we need. This activity will give kids a chance to practice both skills as they describe and guess what a secret object is.

Age Range:	4+
Skills:	Communication, active listening
Materials:	A bag filled with items of various textures, such as textured balls, fruits, and hard and soft toys
Number of Participants:	2+
Where to Play:	Inside, outside, or on video chat (describe the object to a friend or family member from afar!)

BEFORE YOU START
★ Talk about using descriptive language by describing some objects that are visible in your environment. For example, "This pillow feels soft and a little bit bumpy. It's big and squishy. It feels like it would be comfortable to sit on."

HOW TO PLAY
★ Place a secret object in a bag without the players seeing it.
★ One player will reach into the bag and feel the object without looking at it. This player will describe the object to the other players.
★ The other players will listen to the description and guess what the object is.
★ Reveal what the object was, then switch roles for the next object.

THINKING BACK AND LOOKING AHEAD
★ What was hard about this activity?
★ What was fun about this activity?
★ Was it easy or hard to describe the object you were feeling?
★ Were your partner's descriptions helpful? Were you able to guess what the object was based on these?
★ When do you think it would be helpful to use descriptive words when we talk to other people?

TELEPHONE CIRCLE

This familiar game encourages children to listen carefully by tuning in with active listening, and to use an appropriate tone of voice while communicating with others.

Age Range:	4+
Skills:	Active listening, voice levels
Materials:	None
Number of Participants:	5+
Where to Play:	Inside or outside

BEFORE YOU START

* Talk about voice volume and demonstrate what too quiet, too loud, and just right sound like when speaking normally.
* Then, demonstrate what too quiet, too loud, and just right sound like when whispering in someone's ear.

HOW TO PLAY

* All players will sit in a circle.
* For the first round, the adult will start by whispering a secret phrase into the ear of the child to their left. The adult's voice should be quiet enough that the other children in the circle cannot hear the secret phrase but loud enough that the child to the left can.
* That child will then whisper the secret phrase into the ear of the child to their left.
* When the secret phrase reaches the last child, they will say it out loud, and the adult can reveal if the secret phrase was correct!
* Continue this until all the children have had a chance to start a secret phrase for the circle.

THINKING BACK AND LOOKING AHEAD

* What was it like when someone whispered too quietly in your ear? What happened?
* What was it like when someone whispered too loudly in your ear? What happened?
* When is it a good time to use a quiet voice?
* When is it a good time to use a loud voice?

WOULD YOU RATHER

Having conversations with others about their own interests and preferences helps kids develop empathy and expand their social lenses outside of themselves! In this activity, kids will share their own preferences and then practice agreeing or politely disagreeing.

Age Range:	4+
Skills:	Communication, active listening, disagreeing politely
Materials:	None
Number of Participants:	2+
Where to Play:	Inside, outside, or on video chat

BEFORE YOU START

★ Remind the players of a polite way to disagree. Instead of saying, "Ewww, that's gross!" or "What?! You're crazy!" we can say, "I disagree. I like this..." or "I have a different opinion..."

HOW TO PLAY

★ One player will ask a "Would you rather..." question. Players can make their own questions, or use these ideas:
  • Would you rather eat broccoli or carrots?
  • Would you rather play baseball or paint a picture?
  • Would you rather be a dentist or a teacher?
  • Would you rather play a board game or play outside?
  • Would you rather ride a bike or go for a swim?
  • Would you rather live in outer space or under the ocean?
★ One other player will respond.
★ The first player will either say, "I agree. I'd pick that too." or "I disagree. I would prefer to..."
★ Then, the next player will ask a "Would you rather..." question, and another player will answer.

THINKING BACK AND LOOKING AHEAD

* Is it okay to disagree or like different things?
* What's special about having different likes and interests from other people?
* How did it feel when someone disagreed with you? How did they say it?
* How does the way someone disagrees with you affect how you feel?

Part of being a great friend is respecting individual differences. Giving kids opportunities to not only hear friends explain their preferences and choices but also expand on these ideas by sharing their own preferences and choices will help them better understand how people who have different preferences can still get along and be friends.

SNEAK PEEK

Using descriptive communication effectively is so important for being a part of a group or community, because it helps others truly understand what we mean and reduces opportunities for miscommunication or misunderstanding. In this activity, children will practice using descriptive communication to convey an idea to others. They'll also get to practice following directions and using active listening for a fun cooperative activity.

Age Range:	4+
Skills:	Active listening, following directions, communication
Materials:	Blocks
Number of Participants:	2 (or even numbers)
Where to Play:	Inside or outside

BEFORE YOU START

★ Talk about the importance of giving clear instructions. Remind the children that they may need to give one instruction at a time.

★ Talk about how active listening means we have to tune out distractions. Players may want to build their own structures, but they will need to tune out their own thoughts and tune in to their partner's instructions.

HOW TO PLAY

★ Build a block structure prior to starting. It should be hidden from view of the players.

★ Give one player a set of blocks. They should have all the same blocks that are used in the original structure but can also have additional blocks.

★ Another player will get a "sneak peek" at the structure. You can decide how long you will let the player look at the structure (30–90 seconds depending on the ages of the players).

★ Then, the player who got a sneak peek will describe the structure to the player with the blocks.

* The player with the blocks will build the structure based on the instructions from the player who got the sneak peek. The player with the blocks is the only one who is allowed to touch the blocks.
* When the structure is complete, compare it to the original design.

THINKING BACK AND LOOKING AHEAD

* How close was your structure to the original?
* Why do you think it was/was not close to the original structure?
* What helped you (the block holder) focus on the directions?
* What was difficult/easy about giving the instructions? Did you have to change the way you gave instructions to the builder to get the correct results?

FEELINGS CHARADES

This fun acting game will help children practice their nonverbal cues and body language to express emotions. By paying close attention, children will notice facial expressions, body positioning, and movements that relate to feelings to help them identify feelings in others.

Age Range:	5+
Skills:	Nonverbal cues, body language
Materials:	Note cards with feeling words (e.g., "happy," "sad," "embarrassed," "nervous," "scared," "surprised," "angry," "frustrated," "annoyed," etc.) placed in a bowl or bag
Number of Participants:	3+
Where to Play:	Inside, outside, or on video chat

BEFORE YOU START

★ Talk about how you can tell how people are feeling. What clues can you get from their faces? Their shoulders? The way they're sitting or walking?

★ Remind children how facial expressions or body language can tell someone exactly how another person feels without them even saying a word.

HOW TO PLAY

★ Players will take turns being the actor.

★ The actor will draw a note card with a feeling word out of the bowl or bag. (Some players may need help reading the word.)

★ The player will use nonverbal communication to act out the feeling.

★ The other players will try to guess the feeling.

★ After the players guess the feeling, players will share a time they felt that way.

THINKING BACK AND LOOKING AHEAD

★ Which emotions were easy for you to guess? What body language clues did you notice for these emotions?

★ Which emotions were hard for you to guess? What body language clues might you look for in the future?

★ Can you think of a time when you noticed how someone was feeling just by looking at them? What happened?

MOUSE, OWL, BEAR

This activity will help kids understand the differences among passive, aggressive, and assertive communication. Use this activity as a jumping-off point for talking about how the way we say our words may affect others.

Age Range:	5+
Skills:	Communication, assertiveness, voice levels
Materials:	None
Number of Participants:	1+
Where to Play:	Inside or outside

BEFORE YOU START

★ Talk about different types of communication. Each type can be compared to an animal!

Communication Type	What It Is	How It Sounds
Passive (like a mouse)	Passive communication is how we speak to others, or the nonverbal communication we show with our bodies, that says we don't think our needs are as important as others' needs.	"Oh...that's okay; we can do it your way." "Um, that's fine, I guess...."
Assertive (like an owl)	Assertive communication is how we speak to others, or the nonverbal communication we show with our bodies, that says we think our needs are as important as others' needs and that we think other people's needs are as important as ours.	"Actually, I am not comfortable with that." "Can we talk about how we can play fairly?" "Please stop doing that. I don't like it when you touch me." "Can I please have a turn too?"

(continued on next page)

Aggressive (like a bear)	Aggressive communication is how we speak to others, or the nonverbal communication we show with our bodies, that says we think our needs are more important than others' needs.	"We're doing it my way!" "Get out of my way!" "Give it to me now! I want a turn!"

HOW TO PLAY

★ Players will all stand in place.

★ You will say phrases that demonstrate passive, assertive, and aggressive communication. You can use the examples from the chart in the Before You Start section or choose your own.

★ Players will demonstrate with their bodies which type of communication is being used.
  • Passive Mouse: Players will shrink down to a small-body posture and make a squeaking sound.
  • Assertive Owl: Players will gently squat and make owl wings with their arms. They can make an owl-hooting sound with a normal speaking voice.
  • Aggressive Bear: Players will raise their arms above their heads and roar like a bear!

★ Continue this with different phrases so that the players can practice identifying different types of communication.

THINKING BACK AND LOOKING AHEAD

★ How did you feel when I used passive communication?

★ How did you feel when I used assertive communication?

★ How did you feel when I used aggressive communication?

★ Why do you think some people use passive communication?

★ Why do you think it's important to use assertive communication?

★ Why do you think some people use aggressive communication?

TALKING EMOJIS

Using an appropriate tone of voice is so important for social interactions in all settings. This fun emoji activity will help kids tune in to how different emotions affect tone of voice. Use this activity to help kids think about how their own voices sound when they have big feelings, and how others might respond.

Age Range:	5+
Skills:	Communication, tone of voice
Materials:	Cards showing emojis or feelings faces (e.g., happy, sad, angry, scared, silly, etc.)
Number of Participants:	2+
Where to Play:	Inside or outside

BEFORE YOU START
★ Review the emojis or feelings faces on your cards. Practice speaking in a tone of voice that matches each of these emotions before the activity.

HOW TO PLAY
★ Give each player an emoji card or card with a feeling face on it.
★ Say in a neutral tone of voice one of the following phrases:
  • I need to talk to you.
  • I need that block.
  • Where are my clothes?
  • Did you take my book?
  • What's for dinner?
★ Then, each participant will repeat the phrase using a tone of voice that matches the emoji or feeling face on their card. You can choose whether kids will show others what's on their card or if other players will try to guess the emotion.
★ Once everyone has tried, give everyone a new card and try a new phrase!

THINKING BACK AND LOOKING AHEAD
★ Which emotions were most surprising?
★ How do you think people feel when we say things in an angry tone of voice?
★ How do you think people feel when we say things in a sad tone of voice?
★ Why do you think it's important to think about how our words sound before we say them?

SILENT LINES

Everybody line up...silently! In this game, children will organize themselves in lines, based on given categories, using only nonverbal communication. This activity will encourage children to use facial expressions and body language to communicate with others while also tuning in to the cues of others.

Age Range:	6+
Skills:	Nonverbal cues, cooperation
Materials:	None
Number of Participants:	5+
Where to Play:	Inside or outside

BEFORE YOU START
★ Talk about ways that we can communicate without words.

HOW TO PLAY
★ Players will stand together.
★ You will give the players a direction for how they should line up...but the players must line up and arrange themselves silently. For example, you could say:
  • Line up by height.
  • Line up by birthday.
  • Line up by favorite color.
  • Line up by number of siblings.
★ After they have lined up, ask players to share verbally how they lined up and check to see if they are in the correct order.

THINKING BACK AND LOOKING AHEAD
★ What was hard about this activity?
★ What made you laugh during this activity?
★ How did you use your face to communicate?
★ How did you use your hands to communicate?
★ Were there any other ways you found to communicate without using words?
★ Can you think of any times when you might need to communicate without words?

PARTNER MAZE

This a-maze-ing activity will give kids a big social-skills boost! Kids will work together to get through a homemade maze by using effective communication, active-listening, trust, and cooperation skills.

Age Range:	6+
Skills:	Communication, active listening, cooperation, asking for clarification
Materials:	Chairs, pillows, toys, pool noodles, etc.
Number of Participants:	2+ (even numbers)
Where to Play:	Inside or outside

BEFORE YOU START

★ Talk about the importance of giving clear instructions. Remind the children that they may need to give one instruction at a time.
★ Talk about how the child who has closed eyes or is walking backward can ask for clarification if they don't understand the directions.

HOW TO PLAY

★ The adult should set up a maze using household items. You can set this up inside using chairs or pillows or outside using outdoor toys and lawn chairs.
★ Children will work together in pairs. One child will close their eyes while the other child gives verbal directions to get through the maze. Important note: Some children will not feel safe or comfortable closing their eyes. You can also choose to have the child walk backward through the maze with eyes open.
★ When the first child has made it through the maze, partners will switch roles. You may choose to alter the maze slightly since the first partner has already seen the setup.

THINKING BACK AND LOOKING AHEAD

★ Did you bump into the sides of the maze? How did that feel?
★ Which directions were hard to understand? How did you ask your partner to make the directions clearer?
★ Why do you think it's important to ask questions when you don't understand directions?
★ Why do you think it's important to give people clear directions?

THE NUMBERS GAME

This cooperative game requires a lot of active listening and patience. Children will practice tuning in to others' body language as well as to patterns and cooperative practices.

Age Range:	7+
Skills:	Active listening, body language
Materials:	None
Number of Participants:	5+
Where to Play:	Inside or outside

BEFORE YOU START

★ Review the rules in depth and invite players to ask clarifying questions, as this game can be tricky!

★ Talk about nonverbal communication, or the ways that we communicate with others without even saying a word. This could be a facial expression or the way we move or position our bodies. For example:
  • A frown is nonverbal communication that lets us know that someone is feeling sad or upset.
  • Raised eyebrows and a wide-open mouth are nonverbal communication that lets us know someone feels surprised.

★ Ask players to describe how they might know that someone is getting ready to say a number. What might their face look like? What might their body look like?

★ Talk about how players can handle the frustration of having to start over. What might they say or do to make sure the game stays fun for everyone?

HOW TO PLAY

★ All players will sit in a circle.

★ The object of the game is to collaboratively count from 1–30, with each player saying one number at a time. Some other rules:
  • No two players can say the same number simultaneously.
  • Every player must say at least one number.
  • One player may not say two sequential numbers.

- The group cannot set a predetermined order for counting (e.g., the group cannot say, "Let's count in a clockwise circle.").
- If two players say the same number simultaneously, the group must start back at one.
★ The game ends when the group has successfully and collaboratively counted from 1–30.

THINKING BACK AND LOOKING AHEAD

★ How did it feel when you said the same number as someone else at the same time?
★ How did you handle your frustration?
★ What facial clues did you pick up on that helped you know when someone was about to say a number?
★ What body clues did you pick up on that helped you know when someone was about to say a number?
★ What strategies did you use to work together as a group that helped you better understand the nonverbal communication or body language?
★ How did it feel when you finally reached thirty?

LISTENING ORIGAMI

Grab some paper and patience for this listening activity! Children will listen carefully for verbal instructions so that they can create beautiful origami. This activity encourages active listening (and attention to detail too!).

Age Range:	7+
Skills:	Active listening
Materials:	Square paper
Number of Participants:	1+
Where to Play:	Inside

BEFORE YOU START

★ Look online for a simple origami project that you can describe verbally to a child—www.origami-fun.com/origami-for-kids.html is a good place to start.

★ Let all the participants know that they will need to listen carefully for the instructions. Let them know that it's okay if they feel a little bit unsure while they're folding their paper. They should just do their best to fold their paper in the way they understand the directions.

★ It is a good idea to make the origami yourself before starting so that you have something for children to compare theirs to afterward.

HOW TO PLAY

★ Give each participant a piece of square paper.

★ If more than one child is participating, have them sit so that they cannot see each other's paper.

★ Describe the step-by-step instructions for a simple origami design, but do not demonstrate it by folding the paper yourself.

THINKING BACK AND LOOKING AHEAD

★ How did you feel while doing this activity?

★ Take a look at the other participants' papers. Do they all look the same? Why do you think they might be different?

★ What was hard about this activity?

★ What do you think would have made this activity easier?

★ Do you think communication is just about words? What else is important?

....

Talk about how communication involves words *and* actions! Seeing other people's bodies, faces, and movements can help us better understand the words that they are saying. Then, have the children make the origami again while looking at instructions, watching one another, and working together.

....

CHAPTER 3

LISTEN UP! ACTIVE-LISTENING SKILLS

WHAT IS ACTIVE LISTENING?

Active listening is the process of tuning in to a speaker's communication while pushing away thoughts and desires to interject or interrupt. Active listening is all about giving the speaker your full attention, both physically and mentally. There is a component of mindfulness to this skill. Those who actively listen are seeking to fully understand before they respond.

WHAT DOES ACTIVE LISTENING LOOK AND SOUND LIKE?

For younger kids, the focus on active listening involves self-control and self-regulation, as kids need to have calm bodies so that they can tune in to the speaker's words. For older kids, an expansion of active listening can include practice in pushing away thoughts about other things and actively thinking about the words that are being said in the moment. Some examples of what active listening looks like include:

★ A still, calm body
★ Eyes on the speaker
★ Nodding to show you are listening
★ Following directions after listening or following up with a clarifying question
★ Pushing away other thoughts while the person is speaking

ACTIVE LISTENING IN KID-FRIENDLY TERMS

To explain active listening to your kid, say something like this:

When other people are talking, we want to understand what they are trying to tell us. To understand them, we need to really focus on what they are saying. We can do this by using our active-listening skills. Active listening means that we hear what they say and we only think about what they say. We give all our energy and focus to hearing what they have to say! We can do this by keeping our bodies still and calm, looking at them while they speak, and thinking about the words that they are saying. If we need to, we can ask them a question afterward to make sure that we understood what they said.

WHY ACTIVE-LISTENING SKILLS ARE IMPORTANT

Active listening is a skill that will serve kids well in school, in friendships, and beyond. Kids will receive all kinds of information in different settings and be expected to use that information to produce work or demonstrate a skill. Being able to actively listen and then follow directions will be important in the classroom and in extracurricular activities. Active listening will also help kids improve other social skills, like empathy. When they can actively listen to what others are saying without thinking about judgments or criticisms, they are more likely to connect with the person's ideas and experiences.

WHERE AND WHEN KIDS WILL USE ACTIVE-LISTENING SKILLS

Kids will use active listening at home when parents give instructions for chores or routines. They can also actively listen when a friend tells them about the bad day they had yesterday, so that they can respond in a caring way. At school, they will actively listen to lessons from teachers so that they can understand and process the information and follow up with clarifying questions to deepen their understanding. They'll also use active listening in extracurricular activities as coaches or leaders give them instruction on how to try a new skill.

LOOKING AHEAD

In this chapter, you'll find games and activities that ask your child to actively listen by tuning in to words. These activities can be practiced through calm, routine home activities or fun movement-based activities with friends in the neighborhood.

MODEL LISTENER

Even before they are engaging in verbal conversations, you can model the turn-taking conversational technique and active-listening process to babies. Settle in when your baby is active and communicative to show them what it means to be an active listener.

Age Range:	1–2
Skills:	Active listening
Materials:	None
Number of Participants:	Baby and caregiver
Where to Play:	Inside or outside

HOW TO PLAY

★ When your baby is more active (making sounds and movements or other attempts to communicate and engage), strike up a conversation.
★ Make eye contact, nod, and respond to their sounds and movements as if they were verbally communicating with you. Say things like:
  • Wow, really? Is that true?
  • I can't believe that! Thanks for telling me!
  • What happened next? I can't wait to hear!
★ Even though they aren't actually verbally communicating or telling you a story, your attentiveness, eye contact, and responses will model the conversational process to your baby, build connection and security, and give them confidence to keep up the attempts at communication.

THINKING BACK AND LOOKING AHEAD (FOR CAREGIVERS)

★ How did my child communicate with me?
★ How did my child respond to my listening and communication?

ONE-STEP DIRECTIONS

Even the littlest of family members can practice their active-listening skills! Give directions at a developmentally appropriate level to encourage listening and following directions using one-step instructions.

Age Range:	1–2
Skills:	Active listening
Materials:	Varies
Number of Participants:	Toddler and caregiver
Where to Play:	Inside or outside

HOW TO PLAY

★ Give your mobile toddler one-step instructions such as:
  • Pick up the ball.
  • Bring me the ball.
  • Put your cup on the table.
  • Put the book on the shelf.
★ After your child completes the one-step task, give them lots of praise! Offer verbal and physical praise by saying, "Thanks so much for bringing me the ball!" while you pat them on the back, or "You are great at helping! Thanks for putting your cup on the table!" while offering a high five.

THINKING BACK AND LOOKING AHEAD (FOR CAREGIVERS)

★ Which one-step instructions were easy for my child to follow?
★ Which one-step instructions were harder for my child to follow?
★ What other opportunities for practice can we find?

LISTEN UP, LINE CHEF!

Following directions is an essential skill in any venue. Head into the kitchen with some kid-friendly recipes and ingredients, and let the kid lead the way as you give them one-step instructions for creating a culinary delight.

Age Range:	3+
Skills:	Active listening, following directions
Materials:	Kid-friendly recipe, recipe ingredients, kitchen utensils
Number of Participants:	1–2
Where to Play:	Inside

BEFORE YOU START

★ Review kitchen-safety rules. Remind your child that this activity will require active listening, which means they will need to listen carefully to your instructions so that the recipe turns out just how they want it.

★ Consider these recipes ideas based on your child's developmental stage:

Age	Recipe Suggestions
3–4	Turkey and cheese roll-ups Yogurt parfait
5–6	Peanut butter and jelly sandwich Turkey and veggie wrap
7–8	Peanut butter and banana sandwich No-bake protein balls Turkey and cheese–stuffed pitas

HOW TO PLAY

★ Choose a kid-friendly recipe and give your child one-step-at-a-time instructions for getting out necessary ingredients, utensils, etc.

★ Then, give your child one-step-at-a-time instructions for making the recipe.

★ Here's an easy example using simple, one-step instructions for a child aged 5 or older:
- Get the bread from the pantry.
- Get the peanut butter from the shelf.
- Get the jelly from the refrigerator.
- Get a plate from the cabinet.
- Open the bread.
- Take out two slices of bread.
- Put the two slices of bread beside each other on the plate.
- Get a child-safe spreading knife from the drawer.
- Take the lid off the peanut butter.
- Use the knife to get some peanut butter out of the jar.
- Spread the peanut butter on one slice of bread.
- Take the lid off the jelly.
- Use the knife to get some jelly out of the jar.
- Spread the jelly on the other slice of bread.
- Pick up the slice of bread with the jelly.
- Put it on top of the bread with peanut butter so that the jelly and peanut butter are together in the middle.
- Pick it up and take a bite!

THINKING BACK AND LOOKING AHEAD

★ How did it feel to make this yourself?
★ How easy were my directions for you to follow?
★ What would you like to make next?

· ·

Things might get messy at the start, but don't throw in the towell Giving kids continued opportunities for success in this activity (and all the others in this book) will help them develop a sense of competency and self-sufficiency. When kids feel successful in one area, they believe they can be successful in other areas, and they're more likely to try new or difficult tasks and persevere when those tasks seem difficult. So while the kitchen may be messy now, those continued opportunities for success will pay off later in creating competent, persevering kids.

· ·

MOVEMENT CODE WORD

In this activity, kids will have to tune in to a story to listen for key words that encourage them to move their bodies. They'll have to use active listening and self-control at the same time.

Age Range:	3+
Skills:	Active listening, self-control
Materials:	None
Number of Participants:	1+
Where to Play:	Inside or outside

BEFORE YOU START
★ Talk about ways you can actively listen to others, even while moving. For example, you might push other thoughts away, look at their face, and listen carefully to their words. Pay close attention so you don't miss a code word!

HOW TO PLAY
★ Players will stand in their own personal space.
★ In their personal space, players will do some movement that you decide together. This could be jogging in place, arm raises, calf raises, etc.
★ Read the following story. You may choose to pause between sentences for a bit to allow for more movement.

Hi there! My name is Frogger McSwimmington Francine Louise Barbara Hoppytop. I was born down by the lake where all the kids love to swim. They hop out of their cars and run down to the water. Splash! They hop in and start swimming! They swim and swim, laughing while playing in the lake. They hop out of the lake, hop in, and swim again. When they get hungry, they hop out of the water and sit on their picnic blankets to have a snack. This is my chance to swim! I hop from lily pad to lily pad before I land in the water. I swim and swim with the lake all to myself! The children sometimes see me hopping and want to try it too! They hop on the shore, pretending they are frogs. They look a little silly, but I like to watch them hop! After their snack, they hop back in for more swimming! This is my chance to hop on the shore. I love to watch them swim!

★ Anytime the word "swim" is said in the story, players will change their movement to doing swimming arms. Anytime the word "hop" is said in the story, players will change their movement to hopping.

THINKING BACK AND LOOKING AHEAD

★ What was fun about this activity?
★ What happened when you didn't notice one of our code words?
★ What strategies did you use to help yourself listen carefully for the code words?
★ What are some other times when you might need to listen carefully to make sure you don't miss directions?

SHOW-AND-TELL

This is a familiar activity to share something special! Kids will share a favorite meaningful item with others and then tune in to listen about others' favorite items. Use this as an opportunity to practice asking clarifying or meaningful questions about someone else's special something. This can be done in person or on a video chat with friends and family who live far away!

Age Range:	3+
Skills:	Active listening
Materials:	Personally meaningful items
Number of Participants:	2+
Where to Play:	Inside, outside, or on video chat

BEFORE YOU START
★ Talk about what it looks like to be an active listener. Active listeners have still bodies, make eye contact with the speaker, and show that they're listening by nodding. While listening, it's okay to think about a question you might want to ask to learn more.

HOW TO PLAY
★ Participants will take turns telling others about a personally meaningful item.
★ While one person is sharing, the others should listen attentively.
★ After the person has finished sharing, give every child or family member a chance to ask at least one question about what was shared.
★ Continue until everyone has had a turn to share!

THINKING BACK AND LOOKING AHEAD
★ What did you enjoy about this activity?
★ What did you do to be an active listener?
★ What did you learn about someone that you didn't know before today?
★ How does being an active listener help us become closer to the people around us?

LILY PAD TUNES

In this fun movement-based game, kids will practice using their active-listening skills to tune in to the music. They'll also have to use body self-control to keep themselves and others safe as they hop through the game.

Age Range:	3+
Skills:	Active listening, self-control
Materials:	"Lily pads" (items to mark spaces, such as hand towels, throw pillows, pillowcases, etc.), music
Number of Participants:	5+
Where to Play:	Inside or outside

BEFORE YOU START
★ Review the rules and demonstrate how to hop from lily pad to lily pad safely. Remind players to do their best to avoid bumping into others.
★ Talk about what it's like to listen for something while you're playing a game.

HOW TO PLAY
★ Arrange lily pads (towels, pillows, or other items) in a circle. There should be one for each player.
★ Players will squat on their lily pad.
★ Play soft music. It should not be loud, as the goal is for players to really have to be attentive listeners.
★ When the music starts, players will hop like frogs around the circle.
★ While the music is playing, the adult leader will remove one lily pad from the circle.
★ When the music stops, players will stop hopping on the closest lily pad.
★ The player who doesn't have a lily pad will "wade in the pond," and wait in the middle of the circle.
★ Continue this until there is only one frog left!

THINKING BACK AND LOOKING AHEAD
★ Were you able to hear the music stop while you were hopping?
★ What happened when you didn't hear the music?
★ Can you think of a time when you might need to listen for something while you're playing? Why is it important to be able to do this?

EARS, ACTIONS

Test your child's active-listening skills by giving directions while doing something different. This will require them to really tune in to your words and tune out distractions.

Age Range:	4+
Skills:	Active listening, following directions
Materials:	None
Number of Participants:	1+
Where to Play:	Inside or outside

BEFORE YOU START

★ Talk about how active listening means we have to tune out distractions. The movements the adult does might distract players from the words the adult is saying. Players should try to tune out that distraction.

★ You may choose to have players tell you how they might tune out the distraction before the game or wait to see what strategies they try on their own.

HOW TO PLAY

★ Players will stand in front of the adult leader.

★ The adult leader will give verbal action directions such as:

- Stand on your left foot
- Hop on your right foot
- Touch your nose
- Spin in one circle
- Rub your tummy
- Do five jumping jacks
- Hop three times

★ But! While giving verbal action directions, the adult leader should do a different action. For example, if the adult says, "Hop on your left foot," the adult could do three jumping jacks.

★ Players should follow the verbal direction, not the movement the adult is doing.

★ To make the game competitive, players who follow the action the adult is doing rather than the verbal direction can sit for the remainder of the activity. See who is the last one standing!

THINKING BACK AND LOOKING AHEAD

★ What strategies did you use to tune out my distracting movements so you could only focus on my words?

★ What's another situation when you might need to use this strategy?

EARS, BRAINS, ACTIONS

Test your child's active-listening skills using simple sound-based instructions instead of words. Clap once, twice, or three times to give kids a movement instruction. This will require them to really tune in to the sound and tune out distractions.

Age Range:	4+
Skills:	Active listening, following directions
Materials:	Paper and marker (optional)
Number of Participants:	1+
Where to Play:	Inside or outside

BEFORE YOU START

★ Set your movement directions—meaning, what each sound will represent. You can decide on these as a group, or the adult leader can set them. Review and practice the movements a few times before you start.

★ Talk about how this game will require active listening. Players will have to really listen closely to the sound direction to know what to do.

HOW TO PLAY

★ Players will stand in front of the adult leader.

★ The adult leader will give movement directions using sounds such as claps, snaps, or stomps. For example:
  • One clap = hop once
  • Two claps = four overhead claps
  • Three claps = jog in place

★ Plays will need to watch/listen to the sound direction so they know what action to do. (If it would help, you could write down what each direction means for reference.)

★ To make the game more competitive, players who do the wrong action can sit for the remainder of the activity. See who is the last one standing!

THINKING BACK AND LOOKING AHEAD

★ What strategies did you use to help yourself really tune in to the sound direction?

★ What's another situation when you might need to use this strategy?

TOP TEN

Getting to know other people, their interests, their preferences, and their stories is a big part of developing social relationships. In this activity, children will practice listening attentively to others' interests and then test their memories.

Age Range:	4+
Skills:	Active listening
Materials:	Paper and pencil (optional)
Number of Participants:	2+ (even numbers)
Where to Play:	Inside, outside, or on video chat

BEFORE YOU START

★ Talk about ways you can actively listen to others. For example, you might push other thoughts away, look at their face, listen to their words, and think about what they're saying.

★ Remind children that it's okay to ask questions too—this can help us remember what they say!

HOW TO PLAY

★ Give players a category. You can use one of these or make up your own:
  - Ice cream flavors
  - Fruits
  - TV shows
  - TV characters
  - Movies
  - Games

★ Each player will think about their top ten (or five if you are playing with younger children) favorites in the category. If they would like, they can write their lists on paper.

★ One player will share their top-ten list with a partner.

★ The partner will then do their best to tell the rest of the group what was on the list.

★ See how many players can remember! Then, switch roles and play again.

THINKING BACK AND LOOKING AHEAD

★ How many things were you able to remember?

★ When you had things in common on your list, was it easier for you to remember?

★ What active-listening strategies did you try?

★ Why do you think it's important to actively listen when others are speaking?

BUILDING BLOCKS

In this activity, children will have the chance to practice communicating effectively by giving clear instructions on how to build a structure. They'll also get to work on their active-listening skills as they follow directions from others during the building phase.

Age Range:	4+
Skills:	Active listening, following directions, communication
Materials:	Blocks (players should have similar types, numbers, and colors of blocks), something to hide one player's block structure (like a box, a tabletop easel, or something similar)
Number of Participants:	2+
Where to Play:	Inside or outside

BEFORE YOU START

★ Talk about the importance of giving clear instructions. Remind the children that they may need to give one instruction at a time.
★ Talk about how active listening means we have to tune out distractions. Players may want to build their own structure, but they will need to tune out their own thoughts about the design and listen to the leader's instructions.

HOW TO PLAY

★ Give each player a similar set of blocks.
★ Assign one player to be the leader.
★ The leader will build something with their blocks behind a shield that hides their structure from the other players.
★ As the leader builds, they will describe what they are building, giving the other player(s) instructions on how to build the same structure.
★ The other player(s) will try to build a similar structure while listening to the directions.
★ When everyone is done building, reveal the leader's structure and compare. See how close the other player(s) got to the original design.
★ Switch roles and try again.

(continued on next page)

THINKING BACK AND LOOKING AHEAD

★ Did your structures look similar?

★ Why do you think it was/was not close to the leader's structure?

★ What helped you focus on the directions?

★ What would have made this activity easier?

★ Did it get easier when we tried again? Why do you think so?

STOMP, STOMP, WINK

Body language is the name of the game in this activity. Kids will copy the leader's movements, but they'll have to be extra attentive. The leader could transfer the lead with a wink (or a blink, for players who can't wink just yet). Children will practice active listening and body-language awareness in this activity.

Age Range:	4+
Skills:	Active listening, communication
Materials:	None
Number of Participants:	4+
Where to Play:	Inside or outside

BEFORE YOU START
★ Talk about ways you can actively listen to others, even while moving. For example, you could push other thoughts away, look at their face, and watch their movements. Pay close attention so you don't miss a wink!

HOW TO PLAY
★ Players will stand in a circle. One player will be the leader.
★ All other players will copy the leader's movements. The leader can stomp, hop, dance, or simply wave their arms. The leader should stay in their space in the circle as they move.
★ While moving, the leader will transfer the lead to another player by winking (or blinking) at them.
★ When the other player sees the wink, they will become the leader and will choose the movements.
★ The player who transferred the lead will then begin to copy the movements of the new leader.
★ Other players will need to pay attention to movements and recognize that a new player is the leader!
★ Continue playing until everyone has had a chance to be the leader.

THINKING BACK AND LOOKING AHEAD
★ Did you wink at someone and then they didn't notice they were the new leader? What happened?
★ What strategy did you use to make sure you saw a wink?

I TELL, YOU TELL

Learning about each other's lives is a foundational layer of relationships. In this activity, children will practice both sharing their own stories and listening to others' stories.

Age Range:	5+
Skills:	Active listening
Materials:	None
Number of Participants:	2+
Where to Play:	Inside, outside, or on video chat

BEFORE YOU START
★ Talk about what it looks like to be an active listener. Active listeners have still bodies, make eye contact with the speaker, and show that they're listening by nodding.

HOW TO PLAY
★ Give the players a category such as best memory, favorite day, most fun birthday, etc.
★ One child will tell a personal story that fits the category. The child should use lots of details.
★ When the child is done telling the story, ask one of the other children to retell the story they just heard.
★ After they retell the story, ask the first child if the retelling of their story was accurate.
★ Then, let another child tell their own story. Keep playing until everyone has had a chance to tell a story and retell a story.

THINKING BACK AND LOOKING AHEAD
★ How did it feel when someone told your story and got a detail wrong?
★ How did it feel when someone told your story and got the details right?
★ Why do you think it's important to be an active listener when others share details about their lives?

FINISH THE LINE

It's story time...with a twist! Children will work together to create a story, but they'll really have to use those active-listening skills so they can pick up the story in the middle when it's their turn.

Age Range:	5+
Skills:	Active listening
Materials:	None
Number of Participants:	4+
Where to Play:	Inside or outside

BEFORE YOU START

★ Talk about ways you can actively listen to others. For example, you might push other thoughts away, look at their face, listen to their words, and think about what they're saying.
★ Remind kids to pay close attention so they can jump in and make a great story!

HOW TO PLAY

★ Players will sit in a circle.
★ One player will begin telling a story. They will continue until the adult leader says, "Stop!"
★ When the adult leader says, "Stop!" the child who is telling the story will immediately stop midsentence.
★ The player to the left of the child who was telling the story will pick up the story exactly where it was left off, even if it's midsentence.
★ Continue this until all the children have had a chance to add to the story or until the story is complete. The goal is to have a complete story that makes at least some sense.

THINKING BACK AND LOOKING AHEAD

★ Did our story make sense?
★ What strategies did you use to help yourself tune in and pay attention to the story?

TOSS A FAVORITE

Kids will put their listening skills to the test in a fun, active game! Grab a ball, form a circle, and share your favorites in this memory-testing, listening activity.

Age Range:	5+
Skills:	Active listening
Materials:	A soft or squishy ball
Number of Participants:	6+
Where to Play:	Inside or outside

BEFORE YOU START
★ Talk about ways you can actively listen to others. For example, you might push other thoughts away, look at their face, listen to their words, and think about what they're saying.
★ Remind children to pay close attention so they can remember all the names and favorites when it's their turn. Set a goal for how many names and favorites your group will remember!

HOW TO PLAY
★ Players will stand in a circle.
★ Pick a category such as ice cream flavor, animal, movie, TV show, food, etc.
★ One child will hold the ball and say their name and favorite thing from the chosen category. This child will then toss the ball to another child in the circle.
★ The child who catches the ball will say their name and favorite thing from the chosen category *and* the name and favorite thing of the previous person.
★ The next child to catch the ball will say their name and favorite thing and the names and favorite things of everyone who has gone before.
★ Continue doing this until a player is no longer able to recall all the names and favorites or until everyone in the group has had a turn.
★ Try again with a new category.

THINKING BACK AND LOOKING AHEAD
★ Were you surprised by how many we could remember?
★ Which category was easiest? Which category was hardest?
★ What strategies did you use to help yourself be a great active listener?

LEFT-RIGHT PASS

For this game, kids will tune in to a story while tracking movements in the game—so they'll practice active listening while following directions.

Age Range:	5+
Skills:	Active listening, following directions
Materials:	A small item to pass, such as a ball, a small stuffed animal, etc.
Number of Participants:	3+
Where to Play:	Inside or outside

BEFORE YOU START
★ Review left and right for any players who need a refresher.
★ Talk about ways you can actively listen to others. For example, you might push other thoughts away, look at their face, listen to their words, and think about what they're saying.
★ Remind children to pay close attention so they pass at the right time and are ready to receive the item.

HOW TO PLAY
★ Players will sit in a circle.
★ Give one player the small item to pass.
★ Read the following story aloud.

Yesterday, I was looking for just the right shirt to wear for picture day at school! I found my favorite dinosaur shirt, which I left on the floor last week. Uh-oh, I thought. I left this on the floor, so it isn't clean. I can't wear this one. I opened the left drawer in my dresser. Hmm, I thought. This one isn't quite right. I kept looking. That one isn't quite right. That one isn't right either. Halloween shirt? Nope, that's not right either. Will I ever find the right shirt for picture day? I wondered. Wait...down in the bottom-left drawer I thought I spotted something. It was my favorite Hawaiian shirt! It had a surfboard on the left pocket. "This is just the right shirt for picture day!" I

(continued on next page)

exclaimed. I quickly got dressed and went downstairs. "Wow! That's the perfect shirt for picture day. It looks just right," my mom said. I left for school and couldn't wait to have my picture taken!

I went into my classroom and left my things on my desk. I lined up on the left side of the room with my friends. My teacher, Mrs. Harrison, is always silly. She planned a game for us to play while we walked in the hall. "Today, you'll be soldiers as we walk right down the hall! We'll be marching right in our line!" she explained. "Let's go, soldiers! Left right left! Left right left! Left right left! Left right left! Left right left!" We all giggled as we marched right down the hall to have our pictures taken. I gave my biggest, best smile in my just-right Hawaiian shirt. I can't wait to see how my picture turns out. I'm sure it will look just right.

★ Anytime the word "right" is said in the story, the person holding the item will pass the item to the person on their right. Anytime the word "left" is said in the story, the person holding the item will pass the item to the person on their left.

THINKING BACK AND LOOKING AHEAD

★ What happened when someone didn't notice one of our code words?
★ What strategies did you use to help yourself listen carefully for the code words?
★ What are some other times when you might need to listen carefully to make sure you don't miss directions?

BACK-TO-BACK DIRECTED DRAWING

Giving clear instructions can be harder than it sounds! In this activity, one child will give specific, clear instructions for a drawing while the other uses active listening to draw the picture. This activity will give kids a chance to work on their communication skills and hone their patience.

Age Range:	6+
Skills:	Active listening, following directions, calm communication
Materials:	Clipboard, blank paper, pencil, cards with simple drawings (e.g., a tree, a cat, a snowman)
Number of Participants:	2+
Where to Play:	Inside or outside

BEFORE YOU START

★ Talk about what it sounds like to give clear, calm, one-step instructions. Model this for your child. Here's an example: "Pick up the plate from the table. Walk to the kitchen. Set the plate on the counter. Open the dishwasher. Pull out the bottom rack. Place the plate in the bottom rack of the dishwasher. Push the rack back in. Close the dishwasher."

★ Talk about what the artist can say if they need more time. Practice some phrases like, "Can you slow down, please? I'm still drawing the circle. Okay, now I'm ready."

HOW TO PLAY

★ Two players will sit back-to-back. One person will be the artist and the other person will be the instructor.

★ The artist will have a clipboard with a blank piece of paper and a pencil.

★ The instructor will have a card with a simple drawing on it. The instructor will give the artist simple, one-step instructions to draw the image shown on the card. For example, the instructor should not say, "Draw a cat," but should say, "Draw a circle. Add two small triangles on top of the circle."

(continued on next page)

* The goal for the activity is for the artist's drawing to look similar to the instructor's card.
* Switch roles so each player has a chance to be artist and instructor.

THINKING BACK AND LOOKING AHEAD

* How did it feel to be the artist?
* How did it feel to be the instructor?
* What would you do differently next time?
* Why is it important to communicate calmly?
* How did listening carefully help you follow the directions?

Communication is key in this activity! As kids grow in their educational and social settings, they'll have opportunities to give directions to others and explain their thinking. This activity trains kids to slow down as they speak so they can fully and completely explain ideas. This game also encourages empathetic thinking and cooperation, because they will need to think about how their partner is feeling and consider their needs as they speak.

CHAPTER 4

WE'RE ALL IN THIS TOGETHER! COOPERATION SKILLS

WHAT IS COOPERATION?

Simply stated, "cooperation" refers to the ability to work together in a group toward a common goal. Focusing on partner tasks, playing games that are cooperative instead of competitive, and being on a team are great ways for kids to learn these important skills.

WHAT DOES COOPERATION LOOK AND SOUND LIKE?

Cooperation can be demonstrated through words and actions, such as sharing ideas, building upon someone else's plan, or suggesting new strategies. Some other examples of what cooperation looks like include:

★ Working together or alongside one another
★ Offering feedback or making suggestions
★ Sharing materials
★ Making progress toward a common goal

COOPERATION IN KID-FRIENDLY TERMS

To explain cooperation to your kid, try this:

When we play together with someone or work on a project or job together, we help each other. When we work together, things get easier for everyone! Cooperation means that we work together and help each other achieve something. We might be working together to build a really cool Lego set. One person might be great at reading the directions or sorting pieces while the other person is great at putting together small pieces. We can support each other by working together and contributing to the goal. Or we might be cooperating to fold the laundry. Maybe one person will fold the shirts while the other person folds the shorts. Working together helps us get the job done!

WHY COOPERATION SKILLS ARE IMPORTANT

Being able to work together on a team is an essential life skill. Being a helpful, open-minded team member who listens to other people's ideas and accepts feedback about their own ideas helps kids contribute meaningfully in a group setting. Throughout school, sports, extracurriculars, and beyond into adulthood, there will be a need for working with others. Helping kids develop a cooperative mindset early on will encourage them to feel confident about accomplishing tasks with peers or teammates. It will also help them develop a sense of social support and connectedness when others see them as a valuable group member who does their part.

WHERE AND WHEN KIDS WILL USE COOPERATION SKILLS

Kids will use cooperation skills at home, such as when completing a chore with a sibling or in the yard while helping a caregiver plant a garden. They'll use cooperation skills in the neighborhood when the kids team up to build a big fort. When they go to school, they will have daily opportunities to participate meaningfully in groups as cooperative members. As members of a community, your child's cooperation skills may come into play during many group activities, like participating in a community cleanup.

LOOKING AHEAD

In this chapter, you'll find challenges, games, and activities that will require kids to work together. Give them time before their activities to plan and talk over their strategies cooperatively. This planning time will give them opportunities to practice offering and accepting constructive feedback.

CONSTRUCTION CREW

In this cooperative activity, take turns stacking blocks with your child to make a tower. This simple turn-taking activity will help even your littlest learner develop cooperation skills.

Age Range:	1–2
Skills:	Cooperation
Materials:	Stacking blocks
Number of Participants:	Toddler and caregiver
Where to Play:	Inside

HOW TO PLAY

★ Divide the blocks in half and give half to your child and keep half for yourself.

★ Place one block in the middle and say, "My turn."

★ Point to your child's blocks and say, "Your turn! Place a block on the tower." Encourage your child to place just one block.

★ Then, say, "My turn!" Place another block on the tower.

★ Say, "Your turn!" and encourage your child to place a block on the tower.

★ Continue in the "My turn," "Your turn" pattern until you have constructed a tower. If it falls, start again!

★ If your child reaches to place an extra block on the tower, say, "Uh-oh! It's my turn."

★ Offer lots of praise when your child takes their turn and waits for you to take your turn.

THINKING BACK AND LOOKING AHEAD (FOR CAREGIVERS)

★ Was my child able to successfully take turns in this activity?

★ What other turn-taking activities could we try to build this skill?

ROW YOUR BOAT

In this movement-based activity, you and your toddler will work together to row your boat. This simple activity will encourage your child to play cooperatively in a give-and-take manner.

Age Range:	1–2
Skills:	Cooperation
Materials:	None
Number of Participants:	Toddler and caregiver
Where to Play:	Inside or outside

HOW TO PLAY

* Sit cross-legged facing your child. Your child does not need to sit cross-legged and can have legs out straight if that is more comfortable.
* Hold hands in the center.
* Sing, "Row, row, row your boat gently down the stream. Merrily, merrily, merrily, merrily, life is but a dream!"
* As you sing, gently rock back and forth with one person moving forward while the other moves backward and then alternating. Working together to coordinate the rowing movement is the cooperative activity.
* Repeat this several times until your child is no longer interested.

THINKING BACK AND LOOKING AHEAD (FOR CAREGIVERS)

* How did my child do with this cooperative activity? Did they grasp the forward and backward motions?
* What other cooperative activities does my child enjoy? How can we incorporate these into our schedule more often?

YOU PICK, I PICK

Sharing, cooperation, and self-control are the hallmarks of this activity. Participating in activities that others enjoy or choose is a great skill to practice for friendships and will help kids understand that they won't always get to choose the activity or game. Give kids a variety of toys to choose from, and they'll take turns picking one thing for the group to play with together.

Age Range:	2+
Skills:	Cooperation, self-control, respect
Materials:	A collection of preferred toys or games (e.g., blocks, dolls, puzzles, magnet tiles, etc.), timer
Number of Participants:	2+
Where to Play:	Inside or outside

BEFORE YOU START
★ Let the children know that everyone will get a chance to be the person who picks.
★ Talk about how they might play together using each item in the basket so that no one is left out.

HOW TO PLAY
★ Put all the toys or games in a basket. Explain that one child in the group will get to pick what the whole groups plays with.
★ One child will pick something from the basket, and all the children will play with only that for a designated amount of time. You can choose a time interval of 3–10 minutes, depending on the age of the children.
★ Set a timer that the children can see (a sand timer is great for younger children).
★ At the end of the time period, the children will put this toy or game away.
★ Another child will then get to pick what the group plays with for the same designated time interval.
★ Continue this until all the children have had a chance to pick an item.

THINKING BACK AND LOOKING AHEAD
★ How did you feel when you were not the person who got to pick?
★ How did you feel when you were the person who got to pick?
★ How did it feel to be included in playing with what others picked?

LIFEBOAT RIDE

Grab a sheet or a towel for this group activity. This cooperative game will encourage problem-solving skills in kids as they try to fit the whole group aboard the lifeboat.

Age Range:	3+
Skills:	Cooperation, problem-solving
Materials:	A sheet or towel
Number of Participants:	3+
Where to Play:	Inside or outside

BEFORE YOU START
* Talk about how players can share ideas and support one another.
* Let everyone say if they are comfortable with the other players touching them (they might need to hold one another close to all fit). If anyone isn't comfortable with others touching them, remind the other players of this during the game.

HOW TO PLAY
* The object of the game is to fit everyone on the lifeboat.
* Place a lifeboat (sheet or towel) on the floor.
* Players will all sit or stand on the boat. Everyone must be on the lifeboat without any hands or feet touching the ground.
* Once everyone is on, players will step off.
* For the next round, fold the boat so that it is smaller. You can fold a small section or fold it in half depending on the size of your sheet.
* All players will then try to get back on the lifeboat.
* Continue folding the sheet until the players can no longer fit everyone.

THINKING BACK AND LOOKING AHEAD
* What happened when the boat got smaller?
* How did you share ideas with one another?
* How well did you work together?
* How did it feel when others helped you during the game?

CITY PLANNING

This creative adventure has kids pretending to be city planners. They'll design a city using random craft supplies you have on hand. Encourage creative thinking, problem-solving, and communication as they plan how their city will come to life!

Age Range:	3+
Skills:	Cooperation, communication, problem-solving
Materials:	Painter's tape or chalk, tissue boxes, toilet paper rolls, tissue paper, paper, crayons, scissors, glue, other craft supplies, toy vehicles, toy people
Number of Participants:	2+
Where to Play:	Inside or outside

BEFORE YOU START

★ Talk about how the participants might work together for this task. Review how to share your ideas, how to offer feedback, and how to disagree politely.
★ Talk about how they might need to help each other when constructing the buildings for the town, and discuss how to ask for help. This might sound like:
  • I want to make a slide for the playground with the toilet paper roll, but I'm having a hard time getting it to stand up. Can you help me, please?
  • I'm not sure how to make a tree....Do you have any ideas?
  • Where do you think we should put the school?

HOW TO PLAY

★ In this activity, the kids will be city planners and will set up a city using whatever materials you have on hand. For example:
  • Use painter's tape or chalk to create roads for the city.
  • Use tissue boxes for buildings and toilet paper rolls and green tissue paper to make trees, or use paper and scissors to make buildings! Fill up the city with toy vehicles and toy people.
★ You may choose to give the children a list of things to include in the city, such as a school, a grocery store, a park, city hall, ten houses, or other landmarks from your town.

(continued on next page)

THINKING BACK AND LOOKING AHEAD

★ Are you happy with your city?

★ How did you work together?

★ How did you share ideas?

★ How did it feel when someone gave you feedback about an idea?

★ How did you work out any problems that came up?

PARTNER YOGA

Roll out your yoga mats for this cooperative activity. Partner yoga poses are a great way to build cooperative skills and communication skills as kids share how they feel in the poses and share what they need from their partners to feel supported in the poses. Plus, they're working on mindfulness and physical fitness as well.

Age Range:	3+
Skills:	Cooperation
Materials:	Partner yoga cards or a website showing children's yoga poses
Number of Participants:	2+ (even numbers)
Where to Play:	Inside or outside

BEFORE YOU START

★ Review the poses or show your children pictures of the poses online.

★ Talk about moving slowly and safely so that no one gets hurt.

HOW TO PLAY

★ Partners will practice cooperative yoga poses. This requires kids to work together, support each other, and communicate their needs and comfort levels.

★ Try these poses:

- **Seesaw:** Partners sit facing each other with their legs out straight and feet touching. Partners will reach out and hold hands in the middle. One partner will gently and slowly lean back while the other leans forward. Partners will seesaw back and forth, gently stretching and supporting each other.

- **Raindrop:** Partners lie on their backs with their heads touching. Partners will keep their arms at their sides and lift their feet to touch the other person's feet, forming a raindrop shape.

- **Double Boat:** Partners will sit facing each other with their knees bent in toward their abdomens and their toes touching their partner's. Partners will hold hands. Then, partners will try to lift their legs, keeping their toes and feet pressed together. If they can, partners can straighten their legs, lean back a bit, and form a *W* with their double boat shape.

(continued on next page)

THINKING BACK AND LOOKING AHEAD

★ How did you work together?

★ How did it feel to have your partner support you?

★ What might have happened if you hadn't worked together?

During partner yoga, it's important that both partners feel safe and respected. This is a great time to introduce the concept of consent. Show your child how to ask permission before touching others and check in with others to make sure they are still comfortable even after the activity has started. Encourage your child to speak up if they are uncomfortable at any time during the activity. Remind kids that they are in charge of their own bodies and that it's always okay to speak up when they are uncomfortable!

SPACE RACE

This high-energy, cooperative activity is out of this world! Kids will work together to collect rocket fuel for their spaceship. They can communicate throughout the game to encourage one another and offer feedback on strategies being used, which are great skills for any team or cooperative task.

Age Range:	3+
Skills:	Cooperation, problem-solving, self-control
Materials:	Balls, a Hula-Hoop, cones
Number of Participants:	2+
Where to Play:	Outside

BEFORE YOU START
* Let each player practice hopping in and out of the Hula-Hoop.
* Let children give each other feedback or suggestions about how to play—the cooperation can start before the game begins.

HOW TO PLAY
* Spread balls throughout your outdoor space. These are your rocket fuel.
* Set a Hula-Hoop up on cones. This is your spaceship.
* Players will work together to collect rocket fuel for their spaceship.
* Each player may only pick up one piece of fuel at a time.
* When a player picks up a piece of fuel, they must run to the spaceship, hop inside, drop the fuel, and hop out.
* If a player knocks the Hula-Hoop off the cones, you can either restart the game or choose to take one or two pieces of rocket fuel out and return them to the ground.
* The game ends when all the rocket fuel is in the spaceship.

THINKING BACK AND LOOKING AHEAD
* How did you work together for this?
* How did it feel when another player encouraged you?
* What could you do differently if you played again?

BALLOON CIRCLE

This cooperative game is fun for kids of all ages. Circle up and toss some balloons inside the circle. Kids will keep the balloons off the ground using only their feet. This activity encourages teamwork and communication, as kids can talk to encourage one another and talk about what role they will play in the group.

Age Range:	3+
Skills:	Cooperation
Materials:	3 or more balloons
Number of Participants:	4+
Where to Play:	Inside or outside

BEFORE YOU START
★ Give players time to talk about how they will work together for this activity. Let them share some ideas before getting started.
★ Fill balloons with air.

HOW TO PLAY
★ Players will stand in a circle with their arms interlocked (for a large group) or holding hands (for a small group).
★ Put three balloons inside the circle.
★ Players will work together using only their feet to make sure the balloons do not touch the ground.
★ As players are successful, you may choose to add another balloon to the circle.
★ See how long they can keep the balloons in the air, and encourage them to try to beat their time in the next round.

THINKING BACK AND LOOKING AHEAD
★ How did you work together for this?
★ How did you feel when you let a balloon drop?
★ How did you feel when someone else let a balloon drop?
★ How did you encourage one another?

LETTER BODY

In this movement-based activity, kids will work together to use their bodies to make letters. This activity will encourage cooperation and communication as kids share their ideas and offer feedback to each other.

Age Range:	4+
Skills:	Cooperation, communication
Materials:	None
Number of Participants:	2+ (even numbers)
Where to Play:	Inside or outside

BEFORE YOU START
★ Give players time to talk about how they will work together for this activity. Let them share some ideas before getting started.

HOW TO PLAY
★ Children will work with a partner for this activity.
★ Call out a letter.
★ Partners will work together to form the letter with their bodies. They can form the letter while standing, sitting, or lying down.
★ Move through the whole alphabet and see how many letters they can make.

THINKING BACK AND LOOKING AHEAD
★ Which letters were hard to make?
★ Which letters were easy to make?
★ How did you work together for this?

TEAM LIMBO

Let's get ready to limbo! Working together, players will make their way under the bar. They'll have to cooperate to make sure everyone makes it under the bar without letting go of hands or bumping the bar.

Age Range:	4+
Skills:	Cooperation, problem-solving, communication
Materials:	Bar for limbo (such as a broom or mop handle)
Number of Participants:	4+
Where to Play:	Inside or outside

BEFORE YOU START

★ Give players time to talk about how they will work together for this activity. Let them share some ideas before getting started.

HOW TO PLAY

★ Set up a limbo bar on furniture, or have two adults hold the bar.
★ Players will hold hands and work together as a team for the duration of the game.
★ One at a time, each player will move under the limbo bar.
★ If at any point a player touches the limbo bar or any players let go of hands, the team will start over at the beginning.
★ After the group successfully gets under the limbo bar, lower the bar and see if they can do it again!

THINKING BACK AND LOOKING AHEAD

★ What strategies did you use to help one another?
★ How did you feel when you touched the bar or let go of hands?
★ How did you feel when someone else touched the bar or let go of hands?
★ How did you encourage one another?

FINGERTIP HULA-HOOP

Kids will work together to lower a Hula-Hoop without dropping it using only their pointer fingers. This activity will encourage communication as they discuss how they will accomplish the task and talk about their problem-solving strategies.

Age Range:	4+
Skills:	Cooperation, problem-solving, communication, self-control
Materials:	Hula-Hoop
Number of Participants:	3–6
Where to Play:	Inside or outside

BEFORE YOU START
★ Review the rules in depth and show players how to balance the hoop on straight fingers without curling their fingers around the hoop.
★ Give players time to talk about how they will work together for this activity. Let them share some ideas before getting started.

HOW TO PLAY
★ Players will sit (easier) or stand (harder) in a circle.
★ Players will hold their hands out in front of them with palms facing up. They will then close all fingers except for their pointer fingers (each player will have both pointer fingers out).
★ Place a Hula-Hoop on top of the group's pointer fingers. Players should not curl or loop their pointer fingers around the hoop; fingers should remain straight!
★ The object of the game is for players to work together to set the Hula-Hoop on the ground using only their pointer fingers.
★ If the hoop falls or if a player grasps the hoop with their finger, restart at the beginning position.

THINKING BACK AND LOOKING AHEAD
★ How did you feel when you let the hoop drop or curled your finger around the hoop?
★ How did you feel when someone else let the hoop drop or curled their finger around the hoop?
★ What strategies did you use to work together and cooperate?

THREE-LEGGED RACE

This classic picnic favorite is also a fun way to practice social skills like cooperation, problem-solving, and communication. Kids will complete a race with one leg tied to another child's. This activity will help kids practice communicating and working together during a semi-tense situation.

Age Range:	4+
Skills:	Cooperation, problem-solving, communication
Materials:	Bandannas or other material to tie legs together, cones
Number of Participants:	4+ (even numbers)
Where to Play:	Outside (in a grassy spot)

BEFORE YOU START
★ Let partners practice walking a bit with the bandannas on to gain some comfort with their footing.
★ Talk about how they will work together. Let them share some ideas about how they might complete the race.

HOW TO PLAY
★ This activity is best done in the grass in case there are falls.
★ Set up a starting point and ending point for the race, marked with cones (or something similar).
★ With the partners standing side by side and using bandannas or other material, tie the inside legs of the partners together.
★ Partners will begin at the starting point and race to the finish in a three-legged race.
★ To add a layer of difficulty, you can require partners who fall down to start over at the beginning of the race.

THINKING BACK AND LOOKING AHEAD
★ How did you work together?
★ If you fell, how did you handle it?
★ What strategies did you use to help yourselves work together?

OBSTACLE COURSE

Partner up for this fun, cooperative, problem-solving game! Kids will work together to get through an obstacle course, but they'll have to use their communication skills to do it properly. This activity builds teamwork, an essential skill for all areas of life!

Age Range:	4+
Skills:	Cooperation, problem-solving, communication
Materials:	Toys, cones, Hula-Hoops, pool noodles, lawn chairs, or other materials to create an obstacle course
Number of Participants:	2+ (even numbers)
Where to Play:	Outside

BEFORE YOU START
★ Review all parts of the obstacle course so the children know what to do in each section.
★ Talk about how they will work together. Let them share some ideas about how they might approach certain parts of the course.

HOW TO PLAY
★ Set up an obstacle course outside using toys, cones (for weaving in and out), Hula-Hoops (for climbing through), pool noodles (for hopping over), and/or other materials.
★ The goal of this activity is for partners to complete the obstacle course together. They will lock arms either side by side (easier) or back-to-back with both arms locked (harder).
★ If partners knock over part of the course or aren't able to complete a certain obstacle, they should start back at the beginning.
★ If they are able to complete the course easily, challenge them to beat their time!

THINKING BACK AND LOOKING AHEAD
★ How did you work together?
★ How did you handle problems with certain obstacles?
★ What strategies did you use to help yourselves work together?
★ What did you change the second time you went through the course?

PARTNER PROGRESS

This cooperative activity requires focused problem-solving, teamwork, and communication between partners. Kids will work together to complete a task, but they can only use one hand each. This activity may create some frustration, so it is a great way to help kids practice communicating and working together during hard tasks.

Age Range:	5+
Skills:	Cooperation, problem-solving, communication
Materials:	A shoe, a button-down shirt, or a zippered jacket
Number of Participants:	2
Where to Play:	Inside or outside

BEFORE YOU START

★ Talk about how they will work together. Let them share some ideas about how they might complete the task.
★ Talk about what they can do if they feel frustrated during the activity, such as taking deep breaths, encouraging each other, or trying new strategies.

HOW TO PLAY

★ Pick some task for partners to do together, such as tying a shoe, buttoning a shirt, or zipping a jacket.
★ Partners will stand together and interlock their side-by-side arms. Partners should not use these arms while doing this activity.
★ Using their remaining hands, partners will work together to complete the task.

THINKING BACK AND LOOKING AHEAD

★ How did you work together?
★ How did you handle frustration with the task?
★ What strategies did you use to help yourselves work together?

STEM CHALLENGE

Calling all future engineers and architects! In this STEM challenge, children will build problem-solving skills, communication skills, and cooperation skills as they work together to construct famous landmarks using toothpicks and marshmallows.

Age Range:	5+
Skills:	Cooperation, problem-solving, communication
Materials:	Picture of a landmark or building, toothpicks, mini marshmallows
Number of Participants:	2+
Where to Play:	Inside or outside

BEFORE YOU START

★ Talk about how they might work together for this task. Review how to share ideas, offer feedback, and disagree politely. Instead of saying this:
  • Let's put them right here!
  • No, that will never work! Move over and let me do it!
★ Suggest that kids try these approaches instead:
  • What if we tried this...?
  • Hmm, we tried that on this side, and it fell. Maybe we should try it like this....
  • Okay, let's try it that way and see how it goes.

HOW TO PLAY

★ Give or show the participants a picture of a famous building or landmark, like the Eiffel Tower, the Statue of Liberty, or a famous sports stadium.
★ Challenge them to re-create the building or landmark using only toothpicks and mini marshmallows.

THINKING BACK AND LOOKING AHEAD

★ How do you think you did? Does your structure resemble the original?
★ How did you work together?
★ When was it fun? When was it difficult?
★ How did it feel when you got feedback about your idea?
★ What would you do differently next time?

PARTNER STORYBOOK

This activity will encourage cooperation and flexible thinking as kids illustrate their own story and then write the words of someone else's story just by looking at the pictures.

Age Range:	6+
Skills:	Cooperation, flexible thinking
Materials:	Paper, crayons, pencils
Number of Participants:	2+
Where to Play:	Inside

BEFORE YOU START
★ Talk about how you can look at the pictures to figure out what's going on in the story.
★ Discuss potential strategies children can use—will they look at all the pictures before they start writing? Or will they look at one picture at a time?
★ Remind children that the words that are put with their illustrations might not be exactly what they were thinking, and that's okay! We're practicing being flexible and working together.

HOW TO PLAY
★ Fold sheets of paper in half to create a storybook.
★ Give each child a storybook.
★ Children will think about a story they'd like to tell in their storybooks. They will only draw the pictures of the story (no words).
★ After the children have illustrated their stories, they will trade storybooks.
★ Each child will then write words to accompany the illustrations of their partner's story.
★ When everyone is finished, read the storybooks together.

THINKING BACK AND LOOKING AHEAD
★ How easy/difficult was it to figure out what the story illustrations were about?
★ How did it feel to hear the words that were put with your story? Were they close to what you were thinking?
★ Do you like how your story ended up?
★ Did someone add a creative idea to your story?

CROSS THE RIVER

Kids will move across a space while keeping their feet in contact with one another's. It's not as easy as it sounds, though! This activity will encourage kids to talk about effective strategies or share ideas and engage in problem-solving strategies.

Age Range:	6+
Skills:	Cooperation, problem-solving, communication
Materials:	2 jump ropes
Number of Participants:	3+
Where to Play:	Outside

BEFORE YOU START

★ Give players time to talk about how they will work together. Let them share some ideas about how they might cross the river without moving their feet apart.

HOW TO PLAY

★ Place two jump ropes parallel to each other. The space between is your river. The distance between the ropes can be adjusted based on age or after success.
★ Players will stand side by side on one rope.
★ The object of the game is to cross the river as a team.
★ Players will stand so that their feet are touching the feet of the players beside them (players on the outer edges will only be touching one foot to another player). Their feet must remain in contact the entire time! If at any point two feet are no longer in contact, the group must start back at the beginning.
★ The game ends when the team reaches the other side of the river.
★ After the team has made it across the river, you may choose to make the river wider and try again.

THINKING BACK AND LOOKING AHEAD

★ How did you work together for this?
★ How did you feel when your foot lost contact with someone?
★ How did you feel when someone else's foot lost contact?
★ How did you handle frustration during this activity?
★ How did it feel when another player encouraged you?

CHAPTER 5

STEPPING UP! RESPONSIBILITY SKILLS

WHAT IS RESPONSIBILITY?

Responsibility encompasses both the practice of completing tasks that are expected and the act of accepting the results or outcomes of our own actions. It involves doing things that contribute to the family, group, or community by "pulling one's weight" in those areas. As soon as kids are mobile, they can begin to take on responsibilities in the family unit!

WHAT DOES RESPONSIBILITY LOOK AND SOUND LIKE?

The outward demonstration of responsibility changes over time as kids get older and develop maturity. For younger children, responsibility simply looks like doing what they are asked to do or are expected to do, like picking up toys. As kids get older, responsibility still looks like doing what is expected but also includes more self-management behaviors like packing backpacks or managing time and telling the truth. Some demonstrations of responsibility include:

★ Completing chores, like putting away toys and laundry
★ Doing homework
★ Taking care of personal belongings
★ Admitting mistakes
★ Being honest, even when it's hard and there is an expected consequence

RESPONSIBILITY IN KID-FRIENDLY TERMS

To explain responsibility to your kids, try saying something like this:

We all have jobs to do at home, at school, or on our teams. Responsibility means that when you have a job to do, you do it. When you are expected to do something, you step up and do it instead of sitting back and ignoring what needs to be done. It also means that you take control of and take responsibility for your own actions. When you make a mistake, you admit your mistake and try to fix it instead of hiding the mistake or ignoring it. Responsibility means telling the truth and doing what is right.

WHY RESPONSIBILITY SKILLS ARE IMPORTANT

When they are young, kids' responsibilities are found largely at home. They pick up their toys, clean up their messes, and take care of their things. But as kids get older, they will have more responsibilities in more settings. They will be responsible for their school supplies if they attend school outside the home. They will be responsible for taking care of school property and for completing tasks of their own, plus they will have responsibilities to group members at school. They'll be expected to do their part to contribute to outcomes that affect others. If they participate in team sports, they'll have a responsibility to their teammates to show up to practice, work hard, and do their best.

Of course, when they are adults, they'll have more responsibilities that include financial obligations, employment responsibilities and expectations, and more! Starting to teach kids about responsibility early, and gradually adding age-appropriate responsibilities as they get older, will set them up for success in future school, social, and work settings.

WHERE AND WHEN KIDS WILL USE RESPONSIBILITY SKILLS

Kids will have the chance to let their responsibility shine at home, at school, on the sports field, and in the community. When kids learn about responsibility from a young age and feel successful, confident, and competent in their ability to be responsible, they'll feel more comfortable taking on the responsibilities the world will ask of them:

★ They can show they are responsible at school by completing and turning in work on time.

★ They can show they are responsible during extracurricular activities by coming to practices or meetings with a good attitude and trying again even when they make mistakes.

★ They can show they are responsible in the community by picking up after themselves and caring for shared spaces.

Opportunities for demonstrating responsibility will be found everywhere and in increasing levels as kids get older and become more independent and engaged in the world around them.

LOOKING AHEAD

In this chapter, you'll find information on age-appropriate responsibilities, and tips for making responsibilities clear at home so that kids know what's expected and have opportunities for feeling successful. You'll also find helpful tools for monitoring and tracking responsibilities so that kids can begin to self-monitor their responsible behaviors. There are also activities and games that will make home responsibilities fun and help kids practice these skills, which will transfer to a wide variety of settings.

FAMILY EXPECTATIONS

To be responsible, kids first need to know what's expected of them! Circle up the family, grab some paper and markers, and outline the family expectations. Understanding what's expected gives kids the confidence to know they can contribute in positive ways.

Age Range:	2+
Skills:	Responsibility, cooperation, active listening
Materials:	Paper, markers
Number of Participants:	The whole family
Where to Play:	Inside

BEFORE YOU START

★ Talk about how you might phrase your expectations. Try to phrase things in a positive light. For example, instead of saying, "Don't treat each other badly," say, "Treat each other with respect."

HOW TO PLAY

★ Gather the family around the table or an open space.
★ As a family, discuss what is expected of each family member. Consider the following questions:
  • What are we all expected to do?
  • How are we expected to treat each other?
  • How are we expected to talk to one another?
  • How are we expected to treat our belongings?
  • How are we expected to contribute to the family?
★ On a piece of paper, a poster board, or chart paper, write your family expectations.
★ Let everyone sign the expectations as a way to show they are committing to uphold the expectations!

THINKING BACK AND LOOKING AHEAD

★ How will you know when you are meeting the family expectations?

★ How would you like for someone to let you know when you are not meeting the expectations?

★ How will these expectations help our family?

Clear expectations are so helpful for kids! When they know what's expected and what the consequence will be when they don't meet the expectation, they are better able to step up and be a part of the process. Keep expectations as clear and consistent as possible. This will also help kids respect and follow expectations in settings outside the home.

RESPONSIBILITY TRACKER

A visual reference of progress is a great way to help kids stay on track with their responsibilities. Grab some paper, your child's favorite stickers, and a marker to make a responsibility tracker that will help them visually track their progress.

Age Range:	2+
Skills:	Responsibility
Materials:	Stickers, paper, markers
Number of Participants:	The whole family
Where to Play:	Inside

BEFORE YOU START
★ Let kids pick their own stickers or symbol to track their progress.
★ Consider setting a goal for responsibility progress, such as "I will earn fifteen responsibility stickers this week," and celebrate when goals are met. Celebrations don't have to be tangible items; they can be dance parties, movie nights, or cooking a favorite meal together!

HOW TO PLAY
★ Write each family member's name on a piece of paper. Write each person's responsibilities beside their name or in a separate row, as shown in the sample chart.
★ As each person completes their responsibility, add a sticker (or draw a star) by the responsibility so that they can visually reference how they're doing with their responsibilities. Here's an example:

Name	Make Bed		Put Away Dishes		Put Away Laundry		Clean Up Toys	
Keisha								
DeShawn								

THINKING BACK AND LOOKING AHEAD
★ Which responsibilities are easier for you to complete?
★ Which responsibilities are more challenging? What help might you need?
★ What goal do you have for yourself in completing your responsibilities?
★ How will these responsibilities help you contribute to our family?

LAUNDRY SORT

Let the kids tackle that seemingly never-ending mountain of laundry! Kids of all ages can contribute to the laundry responsibility by either sorting or folding. You can even turn this "chore" into a game by challenging your kids to sort under time constraints.

Age Range:	2+
Skills:	Responsibility
Materials:	Laundry, baskets
Number of Participants:	The whole family
Where to Play:	Inside

BEFORE YOU START

★ Designate a space for each laundry stack.
★ Show kids how to fold each type of laundry so they start off on the right foot.

HOW TO PLAY

★ For 2–3-year-olds, challenge them to sort their own laundry into piles of shirts, shorts, pajamas, and socks. They can also match up sock pairs!
★ For kids ages 3–4, challenge them to sort the laundry into piles based on who the laundry belongs to.
★ For kids ages 4+, challenge them to sort *and* fold the laundry.
★ To add a game component, give them a time to beat. Sort the laundry by person in under ten minutes and earn five points. Fold the laundry in under fifteen minutes and earn ten points. Points can earn them a special dance party, a bit of extra screen time, or something else they're motivated to earn.

THINKING BACK AND LOOKING AHEAD

★ What's fun about this activity?
★ Can you think of another way we could turn this into a game?
★ How does this activity help our family?

TOY RELAY

Make cleanup time a breeze with a fun relay! Station one child near a toy box or bin and let another pick up toys and run them to the child near the box. Switch roles halfway through! This activity will not only create a time for cleaning up but will remind kids that working together is their responsibility.

Age Range:	2+
Skills:	Responsibility, cooperation
Materials:	Toys, toy box/bin, timer
Number of Participants:	2+
Where to Play:	Inside or outside

BEFORE YOU START
★ Remove or move any furniture that may be in the path from the play area to the toy box station so that no one trips during the relay.
★ Remind children of how to gently put toys away to take care of their things.

HOW TO PLAY
★ Station one child in the room where toys need to be picked up. Station another child halfway between the first child and the toy box or bin (a grownup can also play this role).
★ Set a timer, and challenge kids to relay the toys from the play area to the child stationed near the toy box and then from that child into the box before time expires.
★ Switch roles halfway through so everyone gets a chance to do each job.

THINKING BACK AND LOOKING AHEAD
★ What was fun about this activity?
★ In what amount of time do you think you could complete the relay next time?
★ How does taking care of and putting away your toys help our family?

Is cleanup time feeling like a huge chore? Are kids complaining about *all* the toys they need to put away? This might be a great opportunity to introduce some empathetic thinking and encourage opportunities for giving. Encourage your child to think about which of these toys they don't play with regularly or would be okay parting with. Ask if they'd be willing to pass these along to some other kids who could enjoy them or who perhaps don't have as many toys as they do. Hand them down to friends or donate them to your favorite local charity.

CHORE CHALLENGE

Kids of all ages are capable of completing chores. Make a list of age-appropriate chores to give your kids an opportunity to demonstrate their responsibility and feel like contributing members of the family.

Age Range:	2–8
Skills:	Responsibility
Materials:	Paper, markers
Number of Participants:	The whole family
Where to Play:	Inside or outside

BEFORE YOU START

★ Review each chore and demonstrate how to complete it. Give kids a chance to try the task and ask questions to make sure they're doing the chore correctly.

HOW TO PLAY

★ Assign age-appropriate chore activities to each family member. Consider these chores, taking into account which ones might be the best fit for your child's individual development and personality:

Age	Appropriate Chores
2–3	Put toys away Put clothes in hamper Stack books on table or put them on bookshelf Mop with a dry mop Dust with a sock or small duster Throw away trash
3–4	Fill pet's bowl Put plastic dishes in dishwasher Make bed Use a handheld vacuum Water plants Carry light grocery bags Dust Sort laundry

5+	Help make lunches
	Organize school materials
	Set table
	Clean room
	Sweep floors
	Load and empty dishwasher
	Vacuum
	Mop with a wet mop
	Fold laundry
	Put away clean laundry
	Make snacks

★ Write each family member's name on a piece of paper and write the chores beside their name (or draw a symbol to represent the chore for younger children).

★ Hang your chore chart in a prominent place so everyone can be reminded of their responsibilities.

THINKING BACK AND LOOKING AHEAD

★ Which chores will be easiest for you to complete?

★ Which chores will be harder for you to complete? What help might you need?

★ How can you help yourself remember to complete your chores?

To pay or not to pay? That is the question! Caregivers often wonder what's best for kids: being paid for their chores or simply being expected to contribute. While this is a personal decision for your household, consider your desired outcome. Do you want kids to develop an understanding of the relationship between work and money? Or do you want them to develop a sense of personal responsibility to their family and community? Research is mixed on what's best, but one thing is certain: Starting early with family chores and expectations fosters a sense of altruism and responsibility in kids!

GARDEN GREEN THUMB

Gardens are a lot of responsibility, but they are rewarding and fun as well. Pick up some seeds and planters, and let your kid create their own garden. Have them plant, then monitor and water the plants as a part of their daily or weekly responsibilities and let them enjoy the fruits of their labors!

Age Range:	3+
Skills:	Responsibility
Materials:	Seeds, potting soil, planters, watering can
Number of Participants:	1+
Where to Play:	Inside or outside

BEFORE YOU START

* Talk to your child about what plants need to grow. They need water, soil, sunlight, and love! You can even encourage your child to speak kindly to their seedlings each day along with watering them.
* Show your child the appropriate amount of water to give the plants that you are growing.

HOW TO PLAY

* Let your child pick out seeds for a plant or plants they'd like to grow.
* Help your child plant the seeds and place them in a spot that gets sunlight.
* Each day, help your child monitor the plants and water them.
* Let older children be responsible for watering on their own. You may even want to make a chart so kids can track this responsibility and mark off each day when they water their plants.
* If your child is growing something edible, let them help prepare a meal or snack using the fruits (or veggies!) of their labor.

THINKING BACK AND LOOKING AHEAD

* What was it like to grow your own plants?
* What was hard about taking care of a plant?
* What was easy about it?
* What would you like to grow next?

PET SPA

Teach kids about the responsibility of pet care in this fun play-based activity! Create your own pet spa and treat your pet to a relaxing bath, nail trim, or brushing. Don't have a pet? Play along with favorite stuffed animals.

Age Range:	3+
Skills:	Responsibility
Materials:	Pet soap, bathtub or hose, calm music, nail file, pet brush, other pet care items
Number of Participants:	1+
Where to Play:	Inside or outside

BEFORE YOU START
★ Remind your child of how to read your pet's feelings and notice when they're uncomfortable.
★ Show your child how to gently give the spa treatments.

HOW TO PLAY
★ Gather supplies for creating your pet spa. Play calming music to create a calm atmosphere.
★ Let your child lead the way in caring for your pet and treating them to a day at the spa. Help them find your pet's brush and then gently brush your pet's fur.
★ If your pet is up for it, help your child give them a gentle massage.

THINKING BACK AND LOOKING AHEAD
★ What was it like to take care of our pet today?
★ What did you notice about our pet's feelings?
★ Why do you think it's important for us to take good care of our pet?

CITY STREET

Help your child develop social responsibility and self-control in this fun movement-based game. They will move around in their space as if they are driving on a city street, watching out for other cars on the road.

Age Range:	4+
Skills:	Responsibility, self-control
Materials:	None
Number of Participants:	3+
Where to Play:	Outside

BEFORE YOU START
★ Review the "in-bounds" area. Remind children that being socially responsible means looking out for others around them by considering how their actions will affect others. It's important to look out for others, think about what others need and how they feel, and take actions that keep them safe.

HOW TO PLAY
★ Designate an "in-bounds" area in which all players need to stay during the game.
★ Call, "Go!" Players will move around in their space as if they are driving cars. They will need to watch out for others and not bump into anyone else.
★ Call, "Stop!" for cars to stop.
★ For an added challenge, change the words that you use. Say, "Watermelon!" for go and "Pineapple!" for stop to encourage active listening while you practice social responsibility and self-control.

THINKING BACK AND LOOKING AHEAD
★ How did you help yourself look out for others while you were driving your car?
★ Why is it important to look out for others when we're moving about in our community?

EGGCELLENT RESPONSIBILITY

Hard-boil some eggs, give them faces and maybe even clothes, and take care of them as if they are babies! Encourage kids to be responsible for their eggs by taking care of them throughout the day and protecting their shells from cracking.

Age Range:	4+
Skills:	Responsibility
Materials:	Supplies for making a bed for the eggs (e.g., tissue box, craft sticks), hard-boiled eggs, supplies for decorating eggs (e.g., markers, googly eyes, yarn and glue for hair, fabric for clothes)
Number of Participants:	1+
Where to Play:	Inside or outside

BEFORE YOU START
★ Create a seat or bed for each egg for easy transport. Talk about ways kids can take care of their eggs and protect them from cracks.
★ If your child will be "paying" someone to babysit, talk about some ways they can pay for services (e.g., raking leaves, vacuuming, dusting, etc.).

HOW TO PLAY
★ Decorate the eggs by giving them faces, hair, and even clothes.
★ Challenge children to take care of their eggs as if they were their babies. Make a list of things babies need, like a morning diaper change and cuddle, breakfast, playtime, a nap, and so forth. Create a schedule for their egg baby!
★ You may choose to set a designated time in which the children will take care of the eggs (for example, for one week) or continue until the eggs crack. Set up the egg baby's bed for naps and bedtime in the refrigerator.
★ For older children, you may choose to add an additional challenge of having them "pay" someone to babysit their eggs. When kids are at school or sports, they can "pay" Grandma to watch the egg in exchange for raking her garden.

THINKING BACK AND LOOKING AHEAD
★ What was challenging about taking care of your egg?
★ What did you learn about the responsibility of taking care of something?
★ What would you do differently if we did this activity again?

ASSEMBLY LINE

Help kids develop an understanding of personal responsibility to a team by setting up a fun, fast-paced assembly line. Put together a toy, wrap sweet treats for neighbors, or make sandwiches in your assembly line to help kids see how each person's role and responsibility are important to the outcome.

Age Range:	4+
Skills:	Responsibility
Materials:	Sweet treat assembly line: baked goods, foil or plastic wrap, ribbon; sandwich assembly line: bread, plates, sandwich ingredients
Number of Participants:	3+
Where to Play:	Inside or outside

BEFORE YOU START

★ Review each step of your assembly line. Talk about how each person has a responsibility for contributing to the final product.

HOW TO PLAY

★ Choose something to assemble in your assembly line. Make sure you have enough jobs for each person to have at least one. If you have more tasks than people, the first person in line can move to the end of the line to complete another task if needed.
★ Set up your assembly line stations. If you are wrapping sweet treats for neighbors, your stations might look like this:
  • Station 1: Wrap treat in foil or plastic wrap.
  • Station 2: Tie a bow on foil or wrap.
  • Station 3: Add a sticker on the wrapped treat.
★ If you are setting up a sandwich assembly line, your stations might look like this:
  • Station 1: Put bread on plates.
  • Station 2: Put peanut butter on bread.
  • Station 3: Put jelly on bread.
  • Station 4: Put bread together with fillings in the middle.
  • Station 5: Cut sandwich in half.

* Set up your stations and assign tasks so that each child or participant has a job.
* Begin your assembly line!

THINKING BACK AND LOOKING AHEAD

* What happened when one part of the assembly line wasn't doing the task (or what would happen if one part of the assembly line wasn't doing the task)?
* Why is each part of the assembly line important?
* How does it feel to have a responsibility to everyone else as a contributor to the final product?

HELPING HANDS

Sometimes responsibility isn't just about doing what's expected—it's about doing a little more to go the extra mile. In this activity, kids will think about ways they can be helpful to their family and how they can contribute at home outside of their regular responsibilities.

Age Range:	4+
Skills:	Responsibility
Materials:	Paper, markers, envelope
Number of Participants:	1+
Where to Play:	Inside or outside

BEFORE YOU START

* Brainstorm ways kids can give extra help at home. You may want to take a walk around the house to help generate ideas visually. Kids may recognize how they can help better when they can see things around the house.
* Talk about social responsibility: It's our job to recognize and ask about the needs of the people around us and help them when we can.

HOW TO PLAY

* Give kids a chance to think about some extra ways they can help around the house.
* On small rectangular pieces of paper, make "Helping Hands Coupons." On the coupons, kids can write or draw ways they can be helpful.
* Place the coupons in an envelope to save for later.
* As kids recognize a need at home or when adults could use a helping hand, coupons can be exchanged for extra help.

THINKING BACK AND LOOKING AHEAD

* How does it feel when you are able to give extra help to someone?
* How do you think giving extra help to someone helps you be responsible?

TIME TRACKER

Visual representations of tasks or times really help kids understand when to do tasks and help them learn the valuable skill of time management! Being able to manage time and complete tasks in a designated time interval will help kids become more responsible and will help them in the future in school.

Age Range:	4+
Skills:	Responsibility
Materials:	Clock or hand-drawn clock, paper, markers
Number of Participants:	1+
Where to Play:	Inside

BEFORE YOU START

★ Make a list of all your child's daily responsibilities. Talk about how long your child thinks each task will take to encourage self-reflection and self-monitoring.

HOW TO PLAY

★ On the clock or hand-drawn clock face, label hours at which certain tasks should be completed. Alternatively, you could make a list of times if children are not accustomed to reading an analog clock.
★ Or your list might look like this:
  • 2:00: Snack
  • 3:00: Homework
  • 4:00: Chores
  • 5:00: Outside
  • 6:00: Dinner
  • 7:00: Bedtime routine

THINKING BACK AND LOOKING AHEAD

★ How will you help yourself stay on track?
★ Which tasks do you anticipate might take less/more time? How will you handle it when you don't complete a task in the time period we chose?

NEEDS DRIVE

Encourage social and community responsibility with this activity as you drive through your community and identify the needs of others. Encourage your child to think about how they can help by brainstorming ideas for small ways to address the need.

Age Range:	4+
Skills:	Responsibility
Materials:	Paper, pencil
Number of Participants:	1+
Where to Play:	Outside

BEFORE YOU START

★ Talk about what social responsibility is: We all have a job or responsibility to care for our community and the people in it. It's up to us to make the community a better place to live in and to help the people who live there.

HOW TO PLAY

★ Go for a drive or walk in your community.
★ Encourage your child to look around and notice needs of the community. Have your child write them down if they are able to. Do this by considering questions like:
  • What does the community need but not have?
  • What would make the community a better place to live in?
  • What problem do you see that would improve the community if it were fixed?
★ When you get home, brainstorm ideas for small ways your child could address the needs you identified. For example, if they noticed that part of the community could use beautifying, they could create artwork or plant flowers to spruce it up.
★ Take action on your small steps. Help your child address the need they noticed, even in small ways.

THINKING BACK AND LOOKING AHEAD

★ How did it feel to take a small step to make the community a better place?
★ What other needs do you think you could address in the community?
★ How can lots of small steps add up to big steps in the community?

ADOPT A NEIGHBOR

Encourage community and social responsibility and empathy in this helpful activity! Choose a neighbor to "adopt" and help your child do small things to brighten that neighbor's day or help them in big and small ways.

Age Range:	4+
Skills:	Responsibility, empathy
Materials:	To be determined by neighbor's needs
Number of Participants:	1+
Where to Play:	Inside or outside

BEFORE YOU START

★ Talk about what the needs of a neighbor might be and how your family can address them nicely. Spend some time thinking about neighbors or people who could use a little extra help or encouragement.

HOW TO PLAY

★ Choose a neighbor or someone in the community to "adopt."
★ Brainstorm ways that your child could help this person or brighten their day. You may choose to let your child interview the person and ask them how they could be helpful or ask the person about their likes and interests.
★ Make a list of things your child plans to do to adopt the neighbor. These things could include:
  • Pulling weeds in their flower beds
  • Raking their yard
  • Dropping off a surprise card or artwork once a week
  • Making dinner for them once a week
  • Spending twenty minutes with the neighbor each week just to talk
★ Help your child put their plan into action.

THINKING BACK AND LOOKING AHEAD

★ How did it feel to help a neighbor?
★ What was the most rewarding part of adopting a neighbor?
★ What else might you like to do to help a neighbor?

SUPER SAVERS

Encourage personal and financial responsibility by setting a goal for kids to earn money to buy things they want. Earning money and buying things on their own will promote a sense of competence and responsibility.

Age Range:	4+
Skills:	Responsibility
Materials:	Paper, marker, piggy bank or envelope
Number of Participants:	1+
Where to Play:	Inside

BEFORE YOU START
★ Talk about the difference between wants and needs. Needs are things that we need to survive, like food, basic clothing, housing, and love. Wants are extra things that we would like to have for fun, entertainment, or enjoyment.

HOW TO PLAY
★ Identify something reasonable that your child wants. Find out how much it costs.
★ On paper, make a graph or thermometer to track your child's earnings.
★ Make a list of extra chores your child can do to earn money for this thing that they want to buy. These should be activities outside of their regular responsibilities or family contributions.
★ As your child earns money, place it in a piggy bank or envelope and track their earning progress on your chart.
★ When your child has earned enough money for the thing they want, take them to buy it!

THINKING BACK AND LOOKING AHEAD
★ What was fun about earning your own money for this item?
★ What was hard about it?
★ How did it feel to earn your own money for this?
★ What did you learn about money and working to earn it?

RESTAURANT ROUNDUP

Working in a restaurant takes a lot of responsibility! Noticing people's needs and responding to requests will help your child develop a sense of responsibility to others. Create your own restaurant at home to practice serving others.

Age Range:	4+
Skills:	Responsibility, attentive listening
Materials:	Play food and utensils or real food and utensils, notepad, pencil
Number of Participants:	3+
Where to Play:	Inside or outside

BEFORE YOU START
★ Talk about the responsibilities of a restaurant server. They greet guests; take drink orders; serve drinks; take food orders; bring extras like condiments, napkins, or silverware; refill drinks; and more.
★ Talk about the attitude servers have in order to make the restaurant experience enjoyable for their guests.

HOW TO PLAY
★ Set up your own restaurant at home.
★ Let your child be the server and play restaurant with siblings or grownups at home. Older children can write down orders of the restaurant guests to serve everyone at once like at a real restaurant. For younger children who are not yet writing, they can either try their best to remember the orders or they can take orders and serve one guest at a time.
★ Use pretend or real food for your restaurant and enjoy the meal!

THINKING BACK AND LOOKING AHEAD
★ What was fun about this activity?
★ Which responsibility was the most difficult?
★ How did it feel to be responsible for our restaurant experience?
★ How will this activity change how you act or engage with others in restaurants in the future?

BALLS IN THE AIR

Practice social responsibility and cooperation in this fun, fast-paced activity! Round up your participants, toss a ball into the circle, and let the fun begin. Kids will keep balls in the air by working together to juggle multiple balls, each child fulfilling their responsibility to the group to keep the balls in the air.

Age Range:	5+
Skills:	Responsibility, cooperation
Materials:	3 or more tennis balls
Number of Participants:	3+
Where to Play:	Inside or outside

BEFORE YOU START

★ Determine the path the balls will follow. Talk about making sure the next person is looking at you before you toss the ball. Practice safe underhand tosses.

HOW TO PLAY

★ Players will stand in a circle.
★ Give one player a tennis ball. The player will toss it to another player, and that player will toss it to the next player. The path the ball follows will stay the same throughout the game. For example, if you are playing with four children, Child 1 tosses to Child 2, Child 2 tosses to Child 3, Child 3 tosses to Child 4, and Child 4 tosses to Child 1 every single time.
★ Continue this pattern with just one ball until the kids get the hang of it. Then, add a second ball into the mix. This ball will follow the same path as the first.
★ As kids get comfortable, add another ball. See how many balls you can add or how many catches kids can get without dropping the balls!

THINKING BACK AND LOOKING AHEAD

★ What was fun or difficult about this activity?
★ What was your responsibility in the game?
★ How did your role affect the other players?
★ What happened to the whole game if one person dropped a ball?
★ What happens when one person doesn't uphold their responsibility? How does it affect others in the family or group?

PRIDE PROJECT

This activity encourages kids to take pride in their responsibilities and progress. They'll prepare a short project or presentation to tell others in the family about their responsibilities and why they take pride in what they do. This activity encourages reflection and a sense of accomplishment.

Age Range:	5+
Skills:	Responsibility, communication
Materials:	Poster board and markers or other art supplies to create a visual representation (your child may also choose to do this project digitally using pictures or slides if they are able)
Number of Participants:	1+
Where to Play:	Inside or on video chat

BEFORE YOU START

★ Talk about your child's responsibilities and ask them which one is most important to them. Talk about why it's important to the family and why they enjoy it.

HOW TO PLAY

★ Each child will choose one or more of their responsibilities that they take pride in and that are important to them.
★ Kids will prepare a short presentation about their responsibility. This could include topics like what the responsibility is, how they do the task, how the task helps the family or community, why it's important, and what they enjoy about doing this task or fulfilling this responsibility. Kids can draw pictures about their responsibilities on poster board, include responsibility trackers they have used to monitor their progress, or write about the experience.
★ Kids can present their pride projects to the family.

THINKING BACK AND LOOKING AHEAD

★ Which responsibility is most important to you?
★ How did it feel to share thoughts about your responsibilities with the family?
★ What does it mean to take pride in your work?
★ Why do you think it's important to take pride in your responsibilities?

CHAPTER 6

I HEAR YOU! EMPATHY SKILLS

WHAT IS EMPATHY?

Empathy is the practice of not only hearing what others are saying but trying to understand how others are feeling. Empathy isn't feeling sorry for someone. Rather, it is feeling along with someone. It doesn't end with understanding, though! Once we step into someone else's shoes, see something from their perspective, and understand how they are feeling, we use that information to guide our actions. So empathy is an active way of responding to others using the information we have gathered from their words, body language, facial expressions, and more.

Empathy is developed and encouraged when kids have strong attachment relationships. When they experience responsiveness and empathy from caregivers, kids are more likely to demonstrate empathy for others. Empathy can be encouraged and expressed in the following ways:

* Challenging stereotypes or prejudices and looking for commonalities
* Trying other people's experiences (walking in their shoes)
* Listening attentively with an open mind and an intention to hear and understand
* Using information from others to make changes

WHAT DOES EMPATHY LOOK AND SOUND LIKE?

The outward demonstration of empathy looks like making efforts to know others and understand their experiences by asking meaningful, nonjudgmental questions and truly listening to their responses. It also includes responding in ways that show understanding as well as changing behavior as necessary. Some examples include:

* Asking meaningful questions about experiences and feelings
* Actively listening by making eye contact and nodding
* Reflecting back what the person has shared and checking for understanding
* Changing behavior or actions as a result of understanding the person better

EMPATHY IN KID-FRIENDLY TERMS

To explain empathy to your kids, try this:

It's really easy to know what you're going through and how you feel. But sometimes other people go through the same thing and have a different feeling. Or they go through things you haven't experienced before. To show others that you care about them and their experiences, you can show them empathy. This means that you try your best to understand what it's like to be them. You try to understand their experiences and their feelings. And then when you do understand how they are feeling, you show them you care by trying to help, by just being with them, or by changing your own behavior to help them feel safe and cared for.

WHY EMPATHY SKILLS ARE IMPORTANT

Being able to tune in to and understand the emotions and experiences of others yields great benefits for individuals and society. Practicing empathy helps kids develop a moral identity or ethical code. When they are able to understand others' experiences, they are more likely to engage in behaviors that serve and honor the needs and rights of others. Empathy also encourages perspective taking and helps kids move away from being egocentric. Kids who are empathetic are better at collaborating and working together in groups because they respect the ideas and experiences that each group member or teammate brings to the table. Empathy creates an environment where others feel safe to share about their experiences and express their needs, because they know others are listening and seeking to understand them.

WHERE AND WHEN KIDS WILL USE EMPATHY SKILLS

Kids will have the chance to demonstrate empathy at home, in school, during extracurricular activities, and beyond. At home, kids can demonstrate empathy by trying to understand what their sibling is going through when they have a disappointing loss in a competition. They can be empathetic when Mom is sad because her best friend moved to another state. Kids can also demonstrate empathy at school when they are surrounded by peers from a variety of backgrounds and experiences. In extracurricular activities, kids can demonstrate empathy for the teammate who has struck out or the gymnast whose dad can't make it to the big meet. In the community, kids can demonstrate empathy by trying to understand what it's like for the elderly woman who is trying to shop from a motorized scooter and cannot reach items on the top shelf.

LOOKING AHEAD

In this chapter, you'll find information on creating an environment at home that values and promotes empathy. You'll also find activities and games that encourage kids to notice how others are feeling and use that information in meaningful ways.

EXTRA EMOTING

Even the youngest kids can learn from an adult modeling emotions during story time or conversations. Pick up your favorite books and really act your heart out in the emotional pieces to help your young child learn about emotions.

Age Range:	1–3
Skills:	Empathy
Materials:	Books
Number of Participants:	1+
Where to Play:	Inside

BEFORE YOU START

★ Choose a book that you know has opportunities for emotional expression. Here are a few suggestions to consider: *Happy Hippo, Angry Duck* by Sandra Boynton; *The Color Monster* by Anna Llenas; *In My Heart* by Jo Witek; and *The Way I Feel* by Janan Cain.

★ Reduce other stimulation in your environment (turn down music or turn off the TV) so that your toddler can really tune in to the story.

HOW TO PLAY

★ Grab your favorite books that have emotional plots or events in them.

★ As you read to your toddler, overexplain the emotions and use overly expressive facial expressions to engage them in the emotional piece of the story. This might sound like, "Oh no! Puppy fell in the puddle! He feels very sad. He's all wet. Look at his sad face and sad eyes! Falling in the puddle makes puppy so sad!"

THINKING BACK AND LOOKING AHEAD (FOR CAREGIVERS)

★ Simply talk to your toddler about the emotions felt in the story. This might sound like, "Puppy felt sad in the story. I feel sad when I fall down too!"

PRETEND PARENTING

Taking care of a doll or stuffed animal is a great opportunity for toddlers to develop empathy as they think about the doll's needs. Spend time playing with a doll and overexplain the doll's feelings and needs to help your child tune in to these needs.

Age Range:	1–4
Skills:	Empathy, responsibility
Materials:	Doll or stuffed animal
Number of Participants:	1+
Where to Play:	Inside

BEFORE YOU START
★ Lay out some items that might be helpful in taking care of the toy (e.g., play food, blanket, change of clothes).

HOW TO PLAY
★ With your toddler, take care of their favorite toy.
★ Explain what the toy needs (e.g., "Dolly is hungry! She feels sad when she is hungry. Let's feed her to help her feel better!" or "Bear is tired. Let's get him ready for bed by reading him a story!").
★ Let your child lead the way in identifying what the toy needs and give them space to take care of it.

THINKING BACK AND LOOKING AHEAD
★ What did your toy need?
★ How did your toy feel?
★ How did you help your toy feel better?

FAMILY CIRCLE

Understanding other people's feelings can start right in the family unit. Circle up for regular family meetings to share and discuss feelings, which will promote understanding and mutual support.

Age Range:	2+
Skills:	Empathy, communication, active listening
Materials:	None
Number of Participants:	The whole family
Where to Play:	Inside, outside, or on video chat

BEFORE YOU START

★ Review the rules of family-circle time. Your rules could include things like:
  • Only one person talks at a time.
  • Everyone gets a chance to share.
  • Everyone's words are important! Show that you care by listening.

HOW TO PLAY

★ Gather the family for regular meetings at a predetermined time. Maybe your family circle will happen at the same time each night or maybe it will happen once a week. Try to commit to a regular time and honor that time to show kids that the practice is important.

★ In your family circle, give everyone a chance to share how they are feeling and how things have been going for them that day or week.

★ While one person is talking, everyone else simply listens. The goal is to promote understanding of one another's experiences.

★ If family members are separated due to work or other circumstances, family circles can take place on video chats too.

THINKING BACK AND LOOKING AHEAD

★ What feelings did you notice as each person talked?
★ How could you tell they felt that way?
★ What is something you learned about one family member or their experience that you didn't know before today?

Making space for genuine communication and family time is important for the whole family. Research also suggests that nonproductive family time (meaning time together in which there is no responsibility-related goal like there is at homework time or chore time) improves emotional and mental well-being for kids and parents alike. This daily five- to ten-minute practice of coming together to share feelings and ideas will give the whole family a boost and keep everyone feeling connected and validated.

PREDICTING CHARACTERS' FEELINGS

Use your regular story time to build empathy skills. In this activity, you'll take time to discuss the characters' feelings and predict how they might feel with alternate events. This will help kids think about how others' actions impact feelings.

Age Range:	2+
Skills:	Empathy
Materials:	Books
Number of Participants:	1+
Where to Play:	Inside or on video chat

BEFORE YOU START
★ Choose books that have strong emotions represented in them (see sidebar).

HOW TO PLAY
★ As you are reading books, pause to ask your child how they think the characters are feeling based on the illustrations and words. Ask them to explain why they think the characters feel this way.
★ Then, ask your child to predict how characters might feel if there were a slight change in the story. For example, "How do you think she might feel if those kids invited her to play instead of ignoring her?" or "How do you think he might feel if he won the race?"

THINKING BACK AND LOOKING AHEAD
★ What helps you know how the characters are feeling?
★ How can you tell how people in real life are feeling?
★ Why do you think it's important to think about how other people are feeling?

If you're looking for some books for this activity, these are some great titles to choose from: *Me and My Fear* by Francesca Sanna; *When Sadness Is at Your Door* by Eva Eland; *The Rough Patch* by Brian Lies; and *After the Fall* by Dan Santat.

MIRROR STORYTELLING

Every face tells a story. Pull out a mirror and let your child tell a highly emotional story while facing the mirror. Ask your child to notice their own facial expressions to build an understanding of how to read other people's emotions as they speak.

Age Range:	3+
Skills:	Empathy
Materials:	Mirror
Number of Participants:	1+
Where to Play:	Inside

BEFORE YOU START
★ Pick a story or experience from your child's past that was highly emotional. Talk about facial-expression features they can notice, like eyes, eyebrows, forehead, mouth, etc.

HOW TO PLAY
★ Give your child a handheld mirror or stand in front of a mounted mirror.
★ Ask your child to tell a story that is highly emotional. You can choose a specific story from your child's experiences or simply ask them to tell a story about a time when they were really angry, excited, frustrated, sad, worried, or shocked. They will tell the story in the mirror.
★ Ask your child to watch their own facial expressions in the mirror as they tell the story and see what they notice.

THINKING BACK AND LOOKING AHEAD
★ What did you notice while you were telling the story?
★ How can paying attention to someone's face while they speak help you understand them better?

MOVIE NIGHT INVESTIGATION

Use family movie night as a way to build empathy. Pause the movie during emotional scenes and ask kids to identify how the characters are feeling and why. This will encourage kids to use facial expressions and body language clues to pick up on how others are feeling.

Age Range:	3+
Skills:	Empathy
Materials:	Movie
Number of Participants:	1+
Where to Play:	Inside

BEFORE YOU START
★ Choose movies that you know have emotional scenes in them. Here are some to consider: *Inside Out, Up, Finding Nemo, Finding Dory, Cinderella*, and any *Toy Story* film.

HOW TO PLAY
★ As you watch a movie together, pause it during emotional scenes.
★ Ask your child to look at the characters' facial expressions and body language. Talk about what is happening in the scene.
★ Ask your child to hypothesize how the characters are feeling in these moments and explain why they think so.

THINKING BACK AND LOOKING AHEAD
★ What was it like to think about how the characters were feeling?
★ How does this help you better understand the movie or the characters' actions?
★ When have you felt like the characters felt? If you haven't, what do you think it would be like to be in that situation?

COMMUNITY CLEANUP

Get the family together for some meaningful community service! Join an organized community cleanup day or create your own. Choose a local park, a beachfront, or even just a section of the street in your neighborhood. Your kid can invite friends and their families to join, or you can make it a family activity. Serving the community will help kids grow in their sense of community responsibility.

Age Range:	3+
Skills:	Empathy, responsibility
Materials:	Trash bags, gloves, trash grabbers, safety vests
Number of Participants:	1+
Where to Play:	Outside

BEFORE YOU START

★ Choose an area of the community to focus your cleanup efforts on if you are organizing this on your own, or find an upcoming cleanup event. Talk to your child beforehand about what you will be doing, what they expect, and why it's important. Review safety rules like wearing gloves, things kids should let adults pick up (like sharp objects or cigarettes), and staying beside an adult, especially if you will be near a street.

HOW TO PLAY

★ Gather your supplies and review how to use each supply (especially if you are using a trash grabber).
★ You may want to take before and after pictures so kids can have a tangible reminder of their efforts!
★ Encourage kids to participate in ways that are appropriate for their age. For example, younger children may carry the trash bag while older kids may be able to use a trash grabber and hold their own bag. As you clean up together, explain what you are doing and why to the kids.
★ Let them ask questions, and provide honest answers about the need for this type of community service and how it best serves the community.

(continued on next page)

THINKING BACK AND LOOKING AHEAD

★ What was fun about this activity today?

★ What questions do you have about what we did or why?

★ What did you think about while we were doing this activity?

★ What other activities would you like to do to serve others?

If a community cleanup project isn't a good fit for your family right now, try one of these at-home service ideas:

• Make a meal for neighbors who have recently had a baby or surgery.

• Go through toys or clothes and choose things to donate.

• Draw pictures for or write letters to residents of a local nursing care facility or pediatric hospital unit.

FAMILY RESOLUTIONS

Taking time to talk through conflicts in the family will go a long way in helping your child develop empathy, communication skills, and active-listening skills that they can apply in every area of life.

Age Range:	3+
Skills:	Empathy, communication, active listening
Materials:	None
Number of Participants:	The whole family
Where to Play:	Inside

BEFORE YOU START
* Remind everyone that they should not interrupt others as they are speaking.
* Remind them how they can show they are actively listening as the other person is speaking by looking at them and nodding.

HOW TO PLAY
* When there is a conflict between family members, bring the whole family together for a family circle, even those who are not directly involved in the conflict. This serves as a reminder that a conflict between only two members of the family can still affect others, as the others overhear parts of the conflict or may feel pulled to side with one member even when they are not directly involved.
* Give each person involved in the conflict a chance to share how they are feeling and their perspective about the situation.
* After all parties have had a chance to share, ask each person involved to share or restate the other's feelings and perspectives about the situation.
* Together, come up with at least two ways to solve the problem or move ahead from the conflict in a positive way.

THINKING BACK AND LOOKING AHEAD
* What was hard about sharing your feelings and perspective?
* What was it like to listen to the other person share their feelings?
* What was it like to recall and retell the other person's feelings and perspective?
* How do you see the conflict differently now that you have heard the other person's perspective?
* What will you do differently in the future?

PET SPOTLIGHT

Pets have feelings too! Take time to think about how pets are feeling to encourage kids to empathize with all the creatures around them.

Age Range:	3+
Skills:	Empathy
Materials:	Pet or friend with a pet
Number of Participants:	1+
Where to Play:	Inside, outside, or on video chat

BEFORE YOU START

★ Talk about how pets might show their feelings. Maybe they'll wag their tails or purr.

HOW TO PLAY

★ Settle in and observe the pet. Encourage your child to notice what the pet is doing, how the pet's face looks, and how the pet's body is moving.
★ Let your child describe your pet's feelings and actions and share why they think the pet is feeling that way.
★ Don't have a pet? Video chat with a friend or family member who does! This is fun even if you do have a pet because your kids can see how other pets feel and act.

THINKING BACK AND LOOKING AHEAD

★ What did you notice about the pet?
★ How did the pet show their feelings?
★ Why do you think the pet is feeling that way?
★ How can you show empathy to the pet? How can you show them you understand and care about them?

EMOJI COMPLETE THE SCENE

This activity combines some creativity with empathy practice. You'll draw an emoji face in the middle of a blank page, and your child will draw the rest of the scene to show why the person is feeling that way. This activity will encourage kids to think about why people experience different emotions.

Age Range:	3+
Skills:	Empathy
Materials:	Paper, crayons or colored pencils
Number of Participants:	1+
Where to Play:	Inside

BEFORE YOU START
★ Talk about reasons people might feel strong emotions. Ask your child to share about times when they've felt each emotion.

HOW TO PLAY
★ On blank paper, draw an emoji or emotion face (happy, sad, angry, scared, surprised, nervous, etc.) in the center of the page.
★ Let your child draw the rest of the picture to complete the scene, showing why the person might feel that way.
★ Let your child explain what they drew and why.

THINKING BACK AND LOOKING AHEAD
★ What was it like to think about how this person was feeling?
★ How did you come up with this idea?
★ What would you do if you were in this situation?

This activity is great for one child to do alone, but get an extra dose of empathetic thinking by doing this with a sibling or friend! Give each child the same emoji and then compare and contrast the scenes they drew. Use this as an opportunity to discuss how, sometimes, the same event can lead to different emotions in different people.

BE THE LAMP

In this silly activity, kids will pretend they are an object in the room and share their perspective from that object's point of view. This activity encourages kids to think about what others might be experiencing outside of their own perspectives.

Age Range:	5+
Skills:	Empathy
Materials:	Paper and pencil (optional)
Number of Participants:	1+
Where to Play:	Inside

BEFORE YOU START

★ Give your child an example. For example, if you picked a trash can, you might say, "People keep putting stinky stuff in me! I'm grumpy because people think I'm only good for holding their trash!" or "I help keep this space clean by holding everyone's trash in one place."

HOW TO PLAY

★ Pick an object in the room (like a lamp, basket, blanket, or trash can).
★ Challenge your child to describe what it's like to be that object from the object's point of view.

THINKING BACK AND LOOKING AHEAD

★ What was fun about this activity?
★ What was it like to think about this object's perspective?
★ How is it different from your perspective?

PERSPECTIVE DETECTIVES

Put your detective hats on for this guessing game! Give one child an emotion and let them tell a story about a time they felt that emotion without saying the emotion itself. Others will try to guess the feeling. This activity will help kids learn to pick up on context clues and really listen to what others are saying as they describe emotional events.

Age Range:	5+
Skills:	Empathy, communication, active listening
Materials:	None
Number of Participants:	2+
Where to Play:	Inside or on video chat

BEFORE YOU START

★ Give kids an example. If the feeling is "angry," the story might sound like this: "I was at the park one day playing Frisbee with my sister. I tossed the Frisbee over her head, and some other kids behind us picked it up. They wouldn't give it back! My face felt really hot and my heart was pounding, and I yelled at them to give our Frisbee back!"

HOW TO PLAY

★ Whisper an emotion word into one child's ear. That child will tell a story about a time when they felt that way, or a time when they might feel that way, without using the emotion word in the story.
★ Other players will be the detectives and listen to the story and try to guess how the person was feeling based on context clues from the story.
★ Continue until everyone has had a turn to tell a story.

THINKING BACK AND LOOKING AHEAD

★ Which emotions were harder to describe without using the word?
★ What clues did you pick up on in each story?
★ How can you use these detective skills in real life when people are telling you about their experiences?

CLASSMATE CLUES

Encourage empathetic thinking all day long, even when kids are at school! In the morning, give your child the name of one classmate. Their job for the day is to notice that classmate and try to figure out how they are feeling. This will help kids grow their empathy as well as develop understanding for others.

Age Range:	5+
Skills:	Empathy
Materials:	None
Number of Participants:	1+
Where to Play:	Inside or outside

BEFORE YOU START

★ Explain that this activity is a way to better understand all the people around them. Remind kids that they don't need to tell anyone about their secret mission, nor should they be staring at the peer all day long. The point is to practice empathy by observing in a compassionate way. They can observe at specific points throughout the day that you determine with your child.

HOW TO PLAY

★ In the morning before school, give your child the name of one classmate. Your child's mission for the day is to notice that classmate and try to figure out how they are feeling at different points during the day. They can observe the classmate at morning arrival, at recess, at lunch, and at dismissal. If your child is in a school with rotating classes, choose 1–2 times during the day when your child will see the classmate. Your child should not tell the classmate or others what they are doing. (If your child does not attend school outside the home, this activity could be done with a teammate or a neighborhood friend as well.)

★ Talk about what your child observed. What body language did they notice? What facial expressions did they see? What events happened around those things?

THINKING BACK AND LOOKING AHEAD

★ What did you notice about this person that you've never noticed before?
★ How are you thinking differently about this person now?
★ What else would you like to know about this person?
★ How could you get to know them and their experiences better?

GRANDPARENT INTERVIEW

Grandparents are a treasure trove of fascinating stories and interesting information! Give your child time to interview a grandparent to get to know them better. This exercise will help expand their empathy and understanding of this family member.

Age Range:	5+
Skills:	Empathy, active listening
Materials:	Paper, pencil
Number of Participants:	At least 1 child and a grandparent or older family member
Where to Play:	Inside, outside, or on video chat

BEFORE YOU START

★ Choose someone to interview. If your child does not have a grandparent, consider interviewing an older neighbor or church member or a friend's grandparent.

★ Find out what your child might like to know about the grandparent or the grandparent's experiences. Talk about questions that are okay to ask (interests, experiences, favorite memories) and those that are not appropriate to ask (money, participation in wars, etc.). You know your family members best and know what will be okay and what will be uncomfortable for them to answer.

HOW TO PLAY

★ With your child, brainstorm and write down a list of interview questions to ask the grandparent. Here are a few questions to consider:
  • What was it like growing up in (city/town/country)?
  • What did you and your siblings do for fun when you were my age?
  • What is something cool that was invented or some new technology that came out when you were a kid?
  • What is your best holiday memory?
  • What activities did you do?
  • What was your favorite meal as a kid?
  • What did you do on family vacations?

(continued on next page)

* If it would make your child more comfortable, practice the interview before the real thing.
* Set up a time for your child to interview the grandparent in person, on the phone, or on a video chat.

THINKING BACK AND LOOKING AHEAD

* What was it like to interview the person?
* What did you learn about them that you didn't know before?
* What did you find you have in common with the person?
* How did this interview change the way you see or think about the person?

IN THEIR SHOES

Encourage your kid to step outside of their own experiences and step into someone else's shoes for this activity. Imagining what it might be like to live a day in the life of someone else will encourage kids to think about the daily experiences of others.

Age Range:	5+
Skills:	Empathy
Materials:	Paper, pencils
Number of Participants:	1+
Where to Play:	Inside

BEFORE YOU START

★ Talk about what the phrase "walk in someone else's shoes" means. This doesn't mean we actually take their shoes and wear them! It means that we think about what it would be like to be that person, what it would be like to live their life, and what it would be like to experience the things that they experience.

HOW TO PLAY

★ Choose a person (real person, book character, or TV character) to be the subject of the activity.
★ Kids will first imagine what it would be like to be this person.
★ Then, kids will write a story about what it would be like to live a day or week in the life of this person.
★ Let kids share their stories.

THINKING BACK AND LOOKING AHEAD

★ What was fun about this activity?
★ What was hard about this activity?
★ While you wrote your story, what did you realize about this person that you hadn't thought about before?
★ Why do you think it's important to consider what it's like to "walk in someone else's shoes"?

PARK PEOPLE WATCHING

Sometimes, building a little empathy can be as easy as sitting back and watching people! Head out to a park, city street, or busy area and watch the people around you. Talk with your child to encourage them to notice things about others and their experiences.

Age Range:	5+
Skills:	Empathy
Materials:	None
Number of Participants:	1+
Where to Play:	Outside

BEFORE YOU START
★ Explain to your kid that you are not there to "talk about" or judge the people you see. You are simply there to notice them and think about what their experiences might be.
★ Remind them how to use a conversational voice so they do not loudly wonder about others in a way that they might overhear. Demonstrate an appropriate voice level for your environment.

HOW TO PLAY
★ Go to a busy area with a place for you to sit.
★ Simply notice the people in the park or on the street. As people pass by, wonder aloud to your child. This could sound like:
  • I see that man walking quickly, and I noticed that his eyebrows are furrowed. I wonder if he is in a hurry or worried about something.
  • That woman and that boy are smiling and laughing. It looks like they are really having fun together.
  • That boy is sitting on the sidelines while the other kids play soccer. I wonder if he is feeling sad or left out.
★ Encourage your child to notice others and verbally point out what they see.

THINKING BACK AND LOOKING AHEAD
★ What did you notice while watching people?
★ Why do you think it's important to take time to notice people around us?
★ How can this help us better understand others?

EMPATHY MAP

An empathy map is a visual representation of things to consider in a situation and ways to show empathy. Kids can use this tool to predict how others are thinking and feeling and then consider what they might say and do to show empathy. Creating an empathy map helps kids really understand what empathy looks like in real life.

Age Range:	5+
Skills:	Empathy
Materials:	Paper, markers
Number of Participants:	1+
Where to Play:	Inside

BEFORE YOU START

★ Brainstorm a list of situations that your kid has seen or noticed at school, during extracurricular activities, or at the park when others might have had strong emotions.

★ Explain that to show empathy, we show others that we understand and care about how they feel. We show them that we care about them and value them as people.

★ Look online for various types of empathy maps.

HOW TO PLAY

★ At the top of the page, write a situation. This can be a made-up situation or something that your kid has actually seen. For example, you might write, "Anna brought kimchi for lunch, and people in our class told her it smelled gross."

★ Draw four squares on the piece of paper, under the situation. Label them "think," "feel," "say," "do."

★ In each of the sections, talk about and write what the person in the situation might *think* and what they might *feel*. Then, write what your child could *say* or *do* to show empathy in the other boxes. Let your child generate these ideas.

THINKING BACK AND LOOKING AHEAD

★ What did you realize about the person in this situation that you hadn't thought about before?

★ How can you show other people that you understand and care about how they feel?

SWITCH SIDES DEBATE

Part of being empathetic is being able to see a situation from someone else's point of view! Start up a friendly debate and then switch sides! Arguing the other side of the debate will help kids expand their perspective, understanding, and empathy.

Age Range:	6+
Skills:	Empathy, communication
Materials:	Paper and pencils (optional)
Number of Participants:	2+
Where to Play:	Inside, outside, or on video chat

BEFORE YOU START

★ Pick your topic, and give kids time to think about their opinions on the topic. You may want to let them write down a couple of ideas for what they will say in the debate. Remind them of how to politely disagree, with statements like, "I hear what you're saying, but I see it this way..." or "That's an interesting point. I think this instead..."

HOW TO PLAY

★ Pick a topic that the kids participating can debate. It could be bedtime, school uniforms, screen time, or something else they are passionate about!
★ Kids will argue for opposite sides of the debate. For example, one might argue that kids need to be in bed by 7:00 p.m. while the other might argue that kids should be allowed to stay up until 8:30 p.m.
★ After kids argue for their points of view in the debate, challenge them to switch positions!

THINKING BACK AND LOOKING AHEAD

★ How did you feel when you shared your own opinions?
★ What was it like to argue the other point of view?
★ What did you realize when you switched sides?
★ Did your perspective change?

CHAPTER 7

JOIN THE FUN! ENGAGEMENT SKILLS

WHAT IS ENGAGEMENT?

"Engagement" refers to one's ability to involve oneself and interact meaningfully with others. Most people find engagement more difficult when meeting people for the first time. For kids, this can look like getting to know new people in new settings or meeting new neighbors. It can also look like joining in on a game with kids they don't know at the park or joining in on a conversation that was already taking place before they arrived.

Being able to engage meaningfully with others gives kids a sense of belonging and social connectedness. It also helps them find commonalities with others as they get to know people and decide if they want to spend more time together. Engagement can be encouraged simply by meeting a variety of new people. Go to the park and meet other kids on the playground. Talk to the family that just moved into the neighborhood. Invite the new student at school over for a playdate. Giving your child ample opportunities to practice engaging with others will help them feel confident and competent as they face new social situations.

WHAT DOES ENGAGEMENT LOOK AND SOUND LIKE?

An outward demonstration of engagement simply looks like talking and interacting with others. This can be a personal conversation or parallel play with a peer. Some examples of outward demonstrations of engagement include:

- ★ Asking others questions about themselves and finding common interests or experiences
- ★ Joining a game others are playing
- ★ Joining a conversation with peers
- ★ Working together with others in meaningful ways

ENGAGEMENT IN KID-FRIENDLY TERMS

To explain engagement to your child, try saying something like this:

There are so many people to talk with, play with, and get to know! You'll meet new people in our neighborhood, at the playground, at school, and in extracurricular activities. It's important to be able to talk to these people, learn more about them, and work together with them in fun ways. "Engagement" is a way to describe how we can talk to people, get to know them, play with them, and work together.

WHY ENGAGEMENT SKILLS ARE IMPORTANT

Being able to talk to others, get to know them, hold a conversation with them, find common interests, and work together are social skills that people of all ages are called upon to use every day. These skills help kids interact with others, especially as they grow and venture outside of the family unit. As kids are able to engage with others, they feel more confident and competent in social settings and experience a sense of belonging and connectedness.

WHERE AND WHEN KIDS WILL USE ENGAGEMENT SKILLS

Simply put, kids will use engagement skills everywhere they interact with peers. Once they begin school or participating in extracurricular activities, kids will be engaging with others independently without coaching from caregivers, so practicing these skills early and often will give them a confidence boost when it's time to navigate these social relationships on their own.

LOOKING AHEAD

In this chapter, you'll find games that encourage kids to discover commonalities with others and activities that help kids work together and value each other's contributions to the group. You'll also find activities to help kids practice joining a game or conversation that started before they arrived—a skill that will certainly come in handy on the playground and in the lunchroom.

ALL ABOARD

In this game, the "conductor" will call out something they like to do or have done, and anyone else who likes that same thing or has done that thing before will climb aboard the train. This activity will help kids recognize things they have in common with others and learn more about each other too.

Age Range:	4+
Skills:	Engagement
Materials:	None
Number of Participants:	4+
Where to Play:	Inside or outside

BEFORE YOU START

Talk about things kids might share, like fun activities they have participated in, things they like to do in their free time, things they like to do at school, or places they have been.

HOW TO PLAY

★ One player will be the train conductor. The conductor will stand up.
★ The other players will be passengers. The passengers will be seated in front of the conductor.
★ The conductor will call out something they like to do or have done before. For example, "I like to play soccer!" or "I went swimming this summer!"
★ If one of the passengers also likes that activity or did that activity too, they will jump up and board the train behind the conductor.
★ You may choose to let each conductor have two or three turns before choosing a new conductor or just do one turn before switching.
★ Continue playing until each player has had several turns.

THINKING BACK AND LOOKING AHEAD

★ What was fun about this activity?
★ How did it feel when people boarded your train?
★ How did it feel when no one boarded your train?
★ What did you learn about someone that you didn't know before today?
★ Why do you think it's important to find things we have in common with one another?

BREAK IN THE GAME

Joining a game with peers is a great skill for kids to have as they get older and move toward independent, non-parent-directed play. In this activity, kids will practice joining a game that others are already playing.

Age Range:	4+
Skills:	Engagement, self-control
Materials:	Varies, depending on game chosen
Number of Participants:	4+
Where to Play:	Inside or outside

BEFORE YOU START

★ Talk about how kids can join a game that others are already playing. Remind them of these strategies:
  • Listen and watch for a few moments to see what the game is and what it's all about. See if it's a familiar game or if you already know the rules.
  • Notice if the game is a two-person game, team game, or individual game.
  • When there is a pause in the game or when the round ends, ask if you can join.
  • If the game is a two-person game, ask if you can play the winner of the game. If it's an individual game, ask if you can join in the next round. If it's a team game, ask if you can join someone's team or swap out with someone in the next round.
  • If you aren't familiar with the game, wait until the round is over and ask someone to teach you how to play.

HOW TO PLAY

★ Pick one person to be the "joiner" first.

★ The joiner will leave the room.

★ The remaining players will start a game. Choose a game that has short rounds so that it is easy for others to join. You could have kids play tic-tac-toe, twenty questions, or even charades.

★ Let the game go on for 1–2 minutes, and then call the joiner in.

★ The joiner's job is to find a way to join the game in an appropriate way and time. This might sound like:
  • Hey, can I join you?
  • Can I play the winner?
  • Can I play in the next round?

★ After the joiner finds a way to join the game and plays a couple of rounds, choose a new joiner. Play until every child has had a chance to be the joiner.

THINKING BACK AND LOOKING AHEAD

★ What was it like to be the joiner?

★ How did it feel to join the game?

★ Did the others make you feel welcome in the game?

★ How could you make others feel welcome joining a game you're playing?

COMMON GROUND

In this timed activity, kids will be challenged to find things they have in common. This game will encourage kids to ask each other questions and engage with one another. This activity is fun to play with people outside of your family, like friends or neighbors.

Age Range:	5+
Skills:	Engagement, communication, active listening
Materials:	Timer, paper and pencils (optional)
Number of Participants:	4+ (even numbers)
Where to Play:	Inside

BEFORE YOU START
★ Brainstorm some ideas for questions kids could ask each other to find things in common. They could ask their partner about their favorite color, food, sport, book, or animal. Or what month their birthday is in, where they were born, or whether they have a pet.

HOW TO PLAY
★ Players will partner up for this activity.
★ Set a timer for five minutes.
★ In five minutes, partners should find at least five things they have in common with each other. If you want, kids can write their commonalities on paper to remember them.
★ At the end of the round, partners will share with everyone else what they have in common.
★ Then, switch partners. Continue until everyone has been partnered with everyone else.

THINKING BACK AND LOOKING AHEAD
★ What did you learn about someone that you didn't know before today?
★ Were you surprised by what you had in common with someone?
★ Why do you think it's important to find things we have in common with each other?

WEAVE A WEB

In this activity, kids will make a visual representation of things they have in common. This game is fun to play with kids outside of the family.

Age Range:	5+
Skills:	Engagement
Materials:	Ball of yarn
Number of Participants:	4+
Where to Play:	Inside or outside

BEFORE YOU START

★ Show players how to hold a strand of yarn with one hand and roll a ball of yarn with the other.
★ Talk about some things they could share about themselves, like their favorite snack, their favorite book, a game they love to play, etc.

HOW TO PLAY

★ Players will sit in a circle.
★ Give one player the ball of yarn. This player will say something that is true about them, such as, "My favorite color is blue." If this is true for any other players, they will say, "Me too!" The player with the yarn will hold the end of the string and roll the ball of yarn to one of the people who said, "Me too!" If no one shares this commonality, the person with the yarn will continue sharing things about themselves until someone shares a commonality.
★ The person who is now holding the ball of yarn will share something about themselves and continue in the same manner.
★ Each player should hold on to the strand (or strands) of yarn they are holding throughout the game, because as the yarn is rolled, the players will weave a web that represents the commonalities among them. Players can receive the ball of yarn more than once.
★ Continue sharing until there is a nice web among the players.

THINKING BACK AND LOOKING AHEAD

★ How did it feel when someone said, "Me too!"?
★ What is it like to look at this web you made? What do you think it means?
★ Why do you think it's important to find things in common with one another?

CONVERSATION CIRCLE

Help kids learn the art of joining a conversation in this activity. Kids will start up a conversation while one player is out of the room. That player will then enter and find a way to join the conversation. This activity will help kids build a very important communication skill that they can use their whole lives.

Age Range:	5+
Skills:	Engagement, communication, active listening
Materials:	None
Number of Participants:	3+
Where to Play:	Inside

BEFORE YOU START

★ Talk about how kids can join a conversation. Remind them of these strategies:
  • Listen for a moment to find out what the conversation is about.
  • Don't jump in right away and interrupt.
  • Find something you can relate to in the conversation.
  • Wait for a break in the conversation to join in.
  • Say something to show how you relate to what they were talking about.

HOW TO PLAY

★ Pick one person to be the "joiner" first. The joiner will leave the room.
★ The remaining players will start a conversation. You may choose to let the kids pick their own topic or give them a topic, such as favorite episode of a show or favorite sport.
★ Let the conversation go on for 1–2 minutes, then call the joiner in.
★ The joiner's job is to find a way to join the conversation in an appropriate way and time. This might sound like:
  • Player 1: My favorite sport is baseball. I love to pitch.
  • Player 2: I like baseball too, but I prefer to play shortstop. I like to field ground balls!
  • Player 1: I've never played shortstop, but I did play first base once.
  • Player 2: I've never played first base, but I have played in the outfield.
  • Player 1: I have played in the outfield too.

- Player 2: I really like to bat, though. That's my favorite part of the game.
- Joiner: Oh, are you talking about baseball? I love playing baseball! I am going to be the catcher this year.

★ After the joiner finds a way to join the conversation, choose a new joiner. Play until every child has had a chance to be the joiner.

THINKING BACK AND LOOKING AHEAD

★ What was it like to be the joiner?
★ How did it feel to join the conversation?
★ Did the others make you feel welcome in the conversation?
★ How can you make newcomers feel welcome in a conversation?

Help your child practice this skill even when they're with adults! Think ahead to when you will be at a playdate or a friend's house and your child will want to talk to you while you're having a conversation with other adults. Create a signal or nonverbal communication strategy to help your child let you know they'd like to speak without interrupting the conversation. Your child could gently touch your arm to communicate that need, or your child could give you a peace sign from across the room. Create a signal that works for you both, and try to respond in a timely manner early on. With practice, your child will be able to wait longer.

SAME, SAME, DIFFERENT

We have things in common, but it's okay to be different too! In this activity, partners will find things they have in common and ways they are different to encourage engagement and conversation.

Age Range:	5+
Skills:	Engagement, communication
Materials:	Timer
Number of Participants:	2+ (even numbers)
Where to Play:	Inside

BEFORE YOU START

★ Talk about some things you could ask your partner to find commonalities, such as your favorite color, food, sport, book, or animal.
★ Remind kids how to politely respond when things are different. For example, they can say, "Oh, that's interesting, I like this instead..." rather than, "What?! That's so weird!"

HOW TO PLAY

★ Players will partner up for this activity.
★ Set a timer for 3–4 minutes.
★ Partners will be challenged to find two things they have in common and one thing that is different about them before the timer goes off.
★ When the timer goes off, partners can share what is the "same, same, different" about them.
★ Switch partners and do it again until each person has had a chance to be partners with everyone.

THINKING BACK AND LOOKING AHEAD

★ What did you learn about someone that you didn't know before today?
★ Were you surprised by what you had in common with someone?
★ Why do you think it's important to find things we have in common with each other?
★ How do the things that make us different help us grow?

CHAPTER 8

DRIVER'S SEAT! SELF-CONTROL SKILLS

WHAT IS SELF-CONTROL?

Self-control is a complex skill that kids develop over time and at different rates. The process of self-control allows kids to slow down and take in information about a situation or environment before they act. It involves being aware of their bodies and their minds as they learn to be in control of their movements and to think about the words they are going to say before they say them. Kids begin learning self-control skills early in life, but these skills continue to develop for a long time—into their twenties!

WHAT DOES SELF-CONTROL LOOK AND SOUND LIKE?

Self-control involves inhibiting actions or behaviors that are inappropriate for the given social setting or context. It looks like being in control of one's body and only expressing words that are kind and appropriate. Some examples of what self-control looks and sounds like include:

* Waiting for a turn on the slide instead of pushing to the front of the line
* Raising a hand and waiting to be called on instead of blurting out
* Keeping unkind thoughts inside instead of saying them aloud

SELF-CONTROL IN KID-FRIENDLY TERMS

To explain self-control to your kid, try this:

> We all have lots of things that we want to do or want to say. But sometimes the things we want to do or want to say aren't okay right now. Our actions might not be appropriate in the place where we are. Our words might hurt someone's feelings or bother people who are working or trying to focus. Self-control means that you are in control of your body, your actions, and your words. It means that you think about the things you want to do and say and decide if they are appropriate in the place where you are right now.

WHY SELF-CONTROL SKILLS ARE IMPORTANT

Self-control is important for socializing, as being able to think about how behaviors or choices will affect those around them helps kids make, develop, and maintain social relationships. Self-control also affects the ways kids are perceived by peers and adults, which can alter the way kids feel about themselves. It can also affect a child's experience at school or in activities. Children who are able to demonstrate self-control at school are more likely to meaningfully engage with the curriculum and with peers, while those who are unable to control their bodies have a harder time focusing on tasks and getting necessary information and instruction.

WHERE AND WHEN KIDS WILL USE SELF-CONTROL SKILLS

There are opportunities for demonstrating self-control in every setting:

* At home, kids can demonstrate self-control by waiting until a parent is finished with that phone call before asking what's for dinner.
* In the neighborhood, kids can show self-control by waiting for their turn in the game instead of taking the ball away from a friend.
* At school, kids can show self-control by sitting appropriately and listening during instruction. They can demonstrate impulse control by using their own materials or asking first to borrow materials instead of grabbing materials from a peer's desk.
* On the sports field, self-control looks like following the game rules instead of fouling a player on the other team.
* Kids can also show self-control in the community by waiting patiently in lines, not grabbing things off shelves in stores, and using appropriate voice levels in public spaces.

LOOKING AHEAD

In this chapter, you'll find games and activities to help kids with important self-control skills like impulse control, body control, delayed gratification, and more. Guide your child to see themselves as in the driver's seat of their actions by learning to stop, take in information from the environment or those around them, think about that information, and then act. It's a learning process, so try to be patient as they learn.

GARAGE BAND

Give each child an "instrument" and make some music. In this activity, kids will practice taking turns, delaying gratification while they wait for a preferred instrument, and following directions while they take cues from the band leader.

Age Range:	2+
Skills:	Self-control, active listening, following directions, sharing
Materials:	A variety of musical instruments or household items that can be used as instruments, such as a pot and a wooden spoon, an empty plastic bottle with rice or beans inside, or a wind chime. Ask kids to help find things throughout the house that can be used as instruments!
Number of Participants:	3+
Where to Play:	Inside or outside

BEFORE YOU START

★ Talk about how band members can listen to the beat of the instrument. Play one instrument and point out the pace of your beat to model this. Show them how to tap the beat with their hand as they listen closely.

★ If you're afraid that the band might argue over certain instruments, remind them that they may not get their first-choice instrument every time, but everyone will get a turn with each instrument as they are passed around.

HOW TO PLAY

★ Each band member will choose one instrument and sit in a circle.

★ Everyone in the band will take turns being the garage band leader. The leader will set the beat for the song, and the other band members will follow the beat with their own instruments.

★ After 1–2 minutes, stop the song. Band members will pass their instruments to the left, and a new garage band leader will be chosen for the next round.

★ Play until everyone has had at least one turn being the garage band leader.

(continued on next page)

THINKING BACK AND LOOKING AHEAD

★ What did you enjoy about this activity?

★ What was hard about it?

★ How did it feel to be the leader?

★ How did it feel to wait for the instrument you wanted?

★ How did you use your body to find the beat of the leader's song?

★ How did you control your body if you felt like you wanted to play your own song?

FREEZE DANCE

In this high-energy game, kids will move their bodies to the music and then exercise their self-control by freezing when the music stops. This activity is great practice for following cues for safe and calm bodies in given situations or environments.

Age Range:	2+
Skills:	Self-control, active listening
Materials:	Music
Number of Participants:	3+
Where to Play:	Inside or outside

BEFORE YOU START
★ Review the rules thoroughly and talk about safely dancing in one's own personal space.

HOW TO PLAY
★ Players will stand in their own personal space for this game.
★ Play music.
★ When the music starts, players will start to dance. They should look out for others to make sure they do not bump into any other players.
★ When the music stops, all players must freeze in their space!
★ Any players who do not freeze within two seconds must sit down.
★ The last player standing is the winner.
★ For added difficulty, keep the music playing and instead call out, "Freeze!" Players will have to actively listen for your voice and control their bodies while they might be tempted to keep dancing to the music.

THINKING BACK AND LOOKING AHEAD
★ What was hard about this activity?
★ What was fun about it?
★ How did you help yourself tune in and listen for the music to stop so you would know when to freeze?
★ How did your body feel when you had to freeze?

CLAP PATTERN

This fun listening game is great way to practice self-control and active listening at the same time. Kids will follow the leader's clapping pattern, which will require them to pay close attention and remain in control of their bodies. See how many steps you can add to your pattern!

Age Range:	2+
Skills:	Self-control, active listening
Materials:	None
Number of Participants:	2+
Where to Play:	Inside or outside

BEFORE YOU START
★ Explain the rules and talk about how players can stay focused on the pattern. Remind them to push away other thoughts and watch and listen carefully.
★ Talk about what players can do if they feel frustrated when they miss part of the pattern: Take a deep breath and try again.

HOW TO PLAY
★ Players will sit in a circle or sit facing the adult leader.
★ In this activity, the adult leader will demonstrate a rhythmic clap pattern that the other players will follow.
★ The adult leader will start a clap pattern. For example, the adult leader might clap and then tap knees. Clap, tap, clap, tap, clap, tap.
★ The other players will follow this pattern.
★ When the players have the rhythm of the movement, the adult leader can add to the pattern. For example, the pattern may change to clap, tap, tap, clap, tap, tap, clap, tap, tap. Continue the new pattern until all players have the rhythm.
★ See how many movements you can add to the pattern!

THINKING BACK AND LOOKING AHEAD
★ How did you help yourself tune in and follow the pattern?
★ How did you feel when you got out of rhythm?
★ How did you help yourself get back on track?

CALMING YOGA SEQUENCE

Yoga is a great activity for practicing self-control. The slow and purposeful movements found in yoga are excellent for teaching body control, body awareness, and focus. Roll out your mats and give these poses a try for a calming self-control boost!

Age Range:	2+
Skills:	Self-control
Materials:	Yoga mats (optional)
Number of Participants:	1+
Where to Play:	Inside or outside

BEFORE YOU START
★ Demonstrate how to do each of the poses. Talk about the importance of moving slowly and staying in control of movements so that no one gets injured.

HOW TO PLAY
★ Use yoga mats or simply spread out on the carpet or grass.
★ Follow this calming yoga sequence that requires kids to remain in control of their bodies:
  • **Corpse pose:** Lie flat on your backs with your arms out by your sides. Stay in this pose, breathing slowly and deeply, for two minutes.
  • **Beginner tree pose:** Come into a standing position. Place your left foot on the inside of your right ankle. Bring your hands together in front of your chest. If you need help with balance, hold your arms out straight, level with your shoulders, making tree branches. Hold this pose for thirty seconds. Switch sides and repeat with the right foot on the left ankle.
  • **Chair pose:** Bring your arms out straight in front of your chest. Slowly bend your knees, pushing your bottom back as if you were about to sit in a chair. Hold this pose for thirty seconds.
  • **Frog pose:** From chair pose, continue lowering your bottom toward the ground into a squatting position with your knees wide apart and hands together in front of your chest. Hold this pose for thirty seconds.
  • **Corpse pose:** Return to corpse pose for some calm, deep breathing. Hold this pose for 2–3 minutes.

(continued on next page)

THINKING BACK AND LOOKING AHEAD

★ How did your body feel in each of these poses?
★ How did you stay in control of your body in these poses?
★ How could you tell if you did not feel in control of your body?
★ How does your body feel after doing this activity?

Research tells us that yoga has a whole host of benefits for kids! Practicing yoga helps kids with emotion regulation and anxiety management. It can also improve kids' body awareness, strength, flexibility, concentration, and memory. Research also suggests that regularly practicing yoga helps kids reduce impulsivity. Making this a regular practice will pay dividends for social, behavioral, emotional, and academic growth!

BALLOON TAP

In this fast-paced activity, kids will exercise their self-control as they tap specific balloons and ignore the others. This game will give kids a chance to practice tuning in to specific tasks while ignoring external distractions, a skill that will come in handy in school.

Age Range:	3+
Skills:	Self-control
Materials:	5–10 multicolored balloons
Number of Participants:	4+
Where to Play:	Inside or outside

BEFORE YOU START
★ Review the rules thoroughly. Remind players of safety rules, like only using their hands for the game.
★ Fill balloons with air.

HOW TO PLAY
★ Players will stand in a circle.
★ Players will tap the balloons back and forth to one another. However, some balloons will be off-limits!
★ Set a rule for which colors of balloons they should tap. For example, they're only allowed to tap the blue and red balloons—not the green and yellow balloons.
★ Players will use self-control to only tap the balloons that are the focus colors.
★ Toss the balloons into the air in the center of the circle and say, "Go!"
★ If a player taps a balloon that's off-limits, they must place one hand behind their back. If they do it again, they must sit down.
★ When the balloons are all on the ground, restart the game. Players who have sat down may rejoin the game.
★ For added difficulty, you can change colors each round.

THINKING BACK AND LOOKING AHEAD
★ What was hard about this activity? What was fun about it?
★ How did you feel when you tapped a balloon that was off-limits?
★ What strategies did you use to help yourself remember which balloons you could tap and which you could not?

FREEZE TAG

This movement-based activity builds on the familiar tag game. However, when kids are tagged, they will have to freeze in the exact position they are in, remaining in complete control of their bodies. This will help kids develop body awareness and self-control.

Age Range:	3+
Skills:	Self-control
Materials:	None
Number of Participants:	4+
Where to Play:	Outside

BEFORE YOU START

★ Explain the rules thoroughly and model for the players how to freeze in place.
★ Show them how to safely and gently tag someone and how to place hands on someone's shoulders to melt them.

HOW TO PLAY

★ Choose one player to be the "icicle." The icicle is "it" and will try to tag the others.
★ If a player is tagged by the icicle, they must freeze in the exact position they're in when they're tagged.
★ Players will stay frozen until another player "melts" them by placing two hands on their shoulders.
★ The game ends when all players are frozen or after a designated amount of time.
★ Play again with a new icicle.

THINKING BACK AND LOOKING AHEAD

★ How did your body feel when you froze in place?
★ How difficult was it to hold your body in that frozen position?
★ How did you control your body to stay in place?

LOUDER, QUIETER

In this activity, children will practice controlling their body-movement intensity—a skill that will come in handy in cooperative play and sports—and their active listening at the same time!

Age Range:	3+
Skills:	Self-control, active listening
Materials:	None
Number of Participants:	2+
Where to Play:	Inside or outside

BEFORE YOU START

★ Demonstrate how to do all the movements. Let players practice how they can do each movement more loudly or more quietly.
★ Ask players to share how they will tune in to make sure they hear the directions during the game.

HOW TO PLAY

★ Players will stand in their own personal space.
★ The adult leader will call out a noise-making movement such as a stomp, clap, snap, etc.
★ Players will start the movement.
★ The adult leader will then call out, "Louder!" or "Quieter!"
★ Players will keep doing the movement but will do it either more loudly or more quietly than they were before.
★ The adult leader can continue with the same noise-making movement and switch between louder and quieter or call out a new movement.

THINKING BACK AND LOOKING AHEAD

★ How did your body feel when you did the movement more loudly?
★ How did your body feel when you did the movement more quietly?
★ Can you think of some other situations or places where we might need to do something more quietly? More loudly?

SIMON SAYS

This old favorite is a great activity for kids to practice active listening and self-control. They will have to tune in closely to the leader's words and distinguish between which instructions to follow and which to ignore.

Age Range:	3+
Skills:	Self-control, active listening, following directions
Materials:	None
Number of Participants:	2+
Where to Play:	Inside, outside, or on video chat

BEFORE YOU START
★ Review the rules. Ask players to share ideas for how they will control their bodies when they hear a command that does *not* start with "Simon says."

HOW TO PLAY
★ Players will stand in front of the adult leader.
★ The adult leader will give commands.
★ Players will only follow the commands that start with "Simon says." You can also choose to use your own name. For example, players should only follow the commands that start with "Mom says," so players would follow the command "Mom says hop on one foot." Players would not follow the command "Hop on one foot."
★ If a player follows a command that does not start with "Simon says," they must sit down.
★ The last player standing is the winner. You may choose to let the winner become the leader.

THINKING BACK AND LOOKING AHEAD
★ How did you help yourself tune in and know which movements to do?
★ How did your body feel when you heard a command that didn't start with "Simon says"?

MIRROR, MIRROR

Mirror, mirror on the wall, who has the best self-control of all? In this game, kids will mirror each other's movements as they tune in to body-language cues and exercise self-control!

Age Range:	3+
Skills:	Self-control
Materials:	None
Number of Participants:	2+ (even numbers)
Where to Play:	Inside or outside

BEFORE YOU START
★ Give kids time to talk about some strategies they might need to use or what might help them be successful in this activity.

HOW TO PLAY
★ Players will stand facing a partner with about 2 feet between them.
★ One player will be the actor, and one player will be the mirror.
★ The actor will move in their personal space or make different facial expressions.
★ The mirror will try their best to be a mirror image of the actor by copying their movements.
★ After a few minutes, switch roles.

THINKING BACK AND LOOKING AHEAD
★ What was it like to be the mirror?
★ What was it like to be the actor?
★ When you were the mirror, what was it like when the actor went too fast?
★ How did your body feel during this activity?
★ What strategies did you use to help yourself be the mirror?

BUCKINGHAM PALACE

Can you make the guard laugh? Can the jester make you laugh? In this game of self-control, kids will take turns trying to make the other person laugh. The object of the game is to keep that laughter inside. This silly activity will give kids practice in controlling laughter in certain situations (even when things might be funny!).

Age Range:	3+
Skills:	Self-control
Materials:	None
Number of Participants:	2+ (even numbers)
Where to Play:	Inside, outside, or on video chat

BEFORE YOU START
★ Watch a video online of the Buckingham Palace guards.
★ Set ground rules for what the jester can and cannot do. For example, the jester should not touch the guard but may sing and make silly faces!
★ Let kids talk about some strategies they might use when they are the guard to help them not laugh at the jester's silly antics.

HOW TO PLAY
★ Players will stand facing a partner with about 2 feet between them.
★ One player will be the guard, and one player will be the jester.
★ The jester's goal is to make the guard laugh, and the guard's goal is to not laugh.
★ If the jester makes the guard laugh, switch roles. If you have more than two players, players can switch partners after two rounds.

THINKING BACK AND LOOKING AHEAD
★ What was it like to be the guard?
★ What was it like to be the jester?
★ When you were the guard, what strategies did you use to help yourself not laugh?
★ Can you think of another time when you might need to use these strategies?

FIVE-COUNT TRIVIA

This trivia game has a twist—kids will take turns answering trivia questions, but they must count to five before responding. This activity will help kids practice exercising self-control and impulse control when it comes to calling out answers (their future teachers will thank you!).

Age Range:	3+
Skills:	Self-control
Materials:	A list of or notecards with questions about a variety of topics (e.g., the family, TV shows, or other topics the participants know a lot about)
Number of Participants:	2+
Where to Play:	Inside or outside

BEFORE YOU START
★ Review the rules and model what it looks like to count to five before answering. Practice counting to five slowly and without rushing.
★ Let players share ideas for how they will remind themselves to count to five before answering the questions.

HOW TO PLAY
★ Read a trivia question from your list or cards.
★ Players *must* count to five before answering the question. Younger players may count aloud, but older players can count silently.
★ If a player blurts out the answer without counting to five, they do not get a point. If a player counts to five and answers incorrectly, they get one point. If a player counts to five and answers correctly, they get two points.
★ The game ends when a player reaches twenty points.

THINKING BACK AND LOOKING AHEAD
★ How did you feel when you realized that you answered without counting?
★ What strategies did you use to help yourself pause and count before answering?
★ Can you think of a time when it might be good to pause for a moment before you say something?

MAY I PLEASE...?

In this game of asking permission, kids will practice first asking and then accepting responses, even if the answer is no. Kids will take turns asking permission to move forward in the game, and the adult leader will grant or deny permission. This is great practice for exercising self-control in situations when kids might not get to do what they want to do.

Age Range:	3+
Skills:	Self-control, active listening, communication
Materials:	None
Number of Participants:	2+
Where to Play:	Inside or outside

BEFORE YOU START

★ Explain the rules, and remind players that the answer can be yes or no.
★ Talk about how they can handle disappointment if the response is no. They can take deep breaths or say, "Okay, maybe next time!"

HOW TO PLAY

★ Players will stand across the room from the adult leader. The object of the game is to get to the adult leader.
★ Players will take turns asking the adult for permission to move forward. They could say things like:
  • May I please hop forward four times?
  • May I please take three steps forward?
  • May I please skip five times forward?
★ The adult leader can respond with "Yes, you may" or "No, you may not."
★ If a player does not start their request with "May I please," they will not get to advance.
★ The game ends when all players have reached the adult leader.

THINKING BACK AND LOOKING AHEAD

★ How did it feel when I said yes?
★ How did it feel when I said no? How did you handle that disappointment?
★ What are some other times when you might ask for something and I might say no? How can you handle your disappointment then?

READY, SET, DANCE

In this fun movement-based game, kids will practice body control and active listening in high-energy situations. The leader will give instructions, but kids will have to really listen carefully while they're moving, because the instructions might be tricky!

Age Range:	3+
Skills:	Self-control, active listening
Materials:	None
Number of Participants:	4+
Where to Play:	Inside or outside

BEFORE YOU START
★ Review the rules. Ask players to share ideas for how they will control their bodies while they listen for the dance and stop commands.

HOW TO PLAY
★ Players will stand in their own personal space.
★ The adult leader will call out, "Ready, set, dance!"
★ Players will stop dancing when the adult leader says, "Ready, set, stop!"
★ Mix up the "dance" and "stop" phrases that you call out with things like:
  - "Ready, set, Dan!"
  - "Ready, set, Daniel!"
  - "Ready, set, dangle!"
  - "Ready, set, dandy!"
  - "Ready, set, Danish!"
  - "Ready, set, style!"
  - "Ready, set, step!"
  - "Ready, set, star!"
  - "Ready, set, stud!"
  - "Ready, set, stew!"
  - "Ready, set, stem!"
★ If you want to make it a competitive game, when a player dances or stops when a different command was given, they will sit down. The last player standing is the winner.

THINKING BACK AND LOOKING AHEAD
★ What was hard about this activity?
★ What was fun about it?
★ How did you help yourself tune in and know what to do?
★ How did your body feel when you heard a statement in which I didn't say "dance" or "stop"?

BALLOON VOLLEYBALL

In this twist on volleyball, kids will practice adapting to changing demands. They'll start out tapping a balloon with both hands, but as the game progresses, they'll only be allowed to use one hand at a time. Being able to adapt to different expectations will help kids in school, sports, and play.

Age Range:	3+
Skills:	Self-control
Materials:	A balloon, something to create a volleyball "net" (e.g., a clothesline or sheet, optional)
Number of Participants:	2+
Where to Play:	Inside or outside

BEFORE YOU START
★ Review the rules and demonstrate how to tap the balloon over the net.

HOW TO PLAY
★ Divide players into two teams. Players will sit on the floor with legs crossed, with each team on opposite sides of the net (the net can be imaginary if need be). Players will play volleyball with a balloon.
★ Start the game by allowing players to tap the balloon over the net with both hands.
★ After players get the hang of this, ask players to sit on one hand to play the game.
★ After players get the hang of that variation, ask them to switch hands.
★ You may choose to keep score. If the balloon lands on the ground, the other team will get a point. If a player pulls their hand out from under their bottom and uses it during the game, the other team will get a point.

THINKING BACK AND LOOKING AHEAD
★ How did your body feel when the balloon came toward you?
★ How did your body feel when the balloon came toward you while you were sitting on a hand?
★ What strategies did you use to help yourself stay in control of your body?

BUMPER CAR CLEANUP

This high-energy game will get kids moving but also require them to be extra atten-tive to their surroundings. In their Hula-Hoop "bumper cars," kids will collect balls, but they'll have to avoid bumping into others! Completing a task while remaining aware of others and maintaining control of their bodies is no easy feat, but practice will benefit them in play, sports, and school situations.

Age Range:	3+
Skills:	Self-control
Materials:	Hula-Hoops (one per child), bucket, 20+ balls or small toys
Number of Participants:	4+
Where to Play:	Outside (in a grassy spot)

BEFORE YOU START
★ Review the rules and remind players they will need to be in control of their bodies and watch out for other players.

HOW TO PLAY
★ Players will all stand inside Hula-Hoops, holding the hoops around their waists. Scatter balls or toys throughout the area. Place a bucket in the area.
★ Players will run throughout the grassy area, picking up one ball or toy at a time and placing it in the bucket.
★ Players should not bump into others while running! If their Hula-Hoops touch anyone else's hoop or body, remove two or three balls or toys from the bucket and return them to the grassy area.
★ The game ends when all the balls or toys are picked up.

THINKING BACK AND LOOKING AHEAD
★ How did it feel when you saw someone coming toward you in their Hula-Hoop?
★ How did it feel when someone bumped into you?
★ How did it feel when you bumped into someone else?

(continued on next page)

* What strategies did you use to help yourself not bump into other players?
* Can you think of other times or situations when you need to be aware of your body and not bump into others?

....

Body control is one of those skills that continues to develop over time. It requires kids to be attuned to their own bodies and the space around them. As they get older, they become better able to integrate sensory information from within and from around them to move and position their bodies safely. If your child has a hard time with this activity at first, that's okay! Using all that sensory information at once is a big task. Keep practicing and giving them opportunities to try.

....

CHAPTER 9

KEEP YOUR COOL! EMOTION-REGULATION SKILLS

WHAT IS EMOTION REGULATION?

"Emotion regulation" is the term used to describe one's ability to recognize and manage feelings. This skill develops over time at different rates for different kids. Newborns lack emotion-regulation skills and rely on their caregivers to help regulate their emotions. As kids receive responsive regulation and guidance in self-soothing, they become better able to cope with feelings like fear, sadness, and anger.

There are several factors that play into regulating emotions. For example, kids need to be able to recognize their emotions. After all, it's pretty hard to deal with a feeling when you aren't sure what feeling is present! This means that kids need to have an awareness of and vocabulary for emotions and what these emotions might feel like in their bodies. When kids can recognize that their stomachs feel full of butterflies and their hearts are pounding and label this with the feeling word "worry," a few things happen. First, the physical experience becomes less scary. Second, they're able to recognize the need for a coping or regulating strategy.

That's why this chapter is important! A major factor in developing emotion regulation is having an awareness of a variety of calming strategies as well as extensive practice in using these strategies.

WHAT DOES EMOTION REGULATION LOOK AND SOUND LIKE?

Emotion regulation will look and sound different for different individuals. When kids practice calming strategies, they find techniques that work for them. All calming strategies don't work well for all kids, and that's okay. Exposure to a wide range of strategies is important so that kids can find regulating strategies that do work for them. In this chapter, you and your child will practice calming and regulating activities that they can use when they notice those big feelings in their body. Some kids will need to talk through big feelings with someone to process what happened and help them move on and feel calm. Others will be fine to take a break by themselves to color, draw, or write in a journal to process their feelings. Still, others may need some time to move around to release the energy and tension they are experiencing as a result of the emotions. Some examples of regulating activities include:

★ Controlled breathing
★ Progressive muscle relaxation
★ Meditation
★ Journaling
★ Exercise
★ Self-talk (such as using a mantra or calming phrase)

EMOTION REGULATION IN KID-FRIENDLY TERMS

To explain emotion regulation to your kid, try this:

Sometimes we have really big feelings. We might feel sad, angry, frustrated, overwhelmed, stressed, or worried. All these feelings are okay to have! We all feel these feelings sometimes, and these feelings can be helpful because they let us know when there might be danger or when things aren't fair. But these feelings can make it hard to think or hard to do what we need to do. Our hearts might pump faster. We might breathe more quickly. Our bellies might hurt or feel full of butterflies. It might be really hard to think or gather our thoughts.

When this happens, it's important to have strategies you can use to help yourself feel better. When your body and mind are keyed up and feel like they're racing, it's like when a car is driving as fast as it can! The engine is roaring and the car is difficult to steer. If we don't slow down the car, the engine could overheat or the car could crash. People might get hurt. We need to find a way to slow the car down and cool the engine.

Sometimes our bodies can feel like that roaring engine. We need to do things to help our bodies feel calmer and cooler. You can try things like breathing slowly. You can exercise to let go of some of the revved-up energy. You can write or draw about your feelings. There are lots of ways you can deal with big feelings so that your body and mind can feel calmer and you can get back to doing what you need to do and want to do to have fun!

WHY EMOTION-REGULATION SKILLS ARE IMPORTANT

Emotions are useful responses that help us understand events and experiences around us in the world. But when the physical experiences of emotions are leading the way, it's hard to think, plan, and function appropriately. For example, it's really difficult to complete schoolwork or participate meaningfully in a group of peers when anger is leading our actions. Being able to recognize and regulate emotions is an important skill for kids (and adults) to practice and develop so that they can make decisions, plan actions, communicate, and interact with peers in positive ways.

WHERE AND WHEN KIDS WILL USE EMOTION-REGULATION SKILLS

Kids will use emotion regulation at home when they have a disagreement with a sibling, in a sporting event when someone isn't playing fair, at school when group members disagree about how to complete the project, and even in the grocery store when Mom says no to buying ice cream. In general, these skills come in handy when things aren't fair, when things are disappointing, when others aren't kind, when things are really exciting and overstimulating, and when things are scary.

LOOKING AHEAD

In this chapter, you'll find information on helping babies and children alike develop age-appropriate emotion regulation. You'll learn how modeling caregiver responsiveness, establishing routines to create safety and boundaries for kids, setting up a calm space in your home where kids can take a break to regulate, and introducing activities to practice will all help kids be ready to implement calming strategies when needed!

RESPONSIVE REGULATION

While infants are completely dependent on their caregivers to meet their every need, the ways that caregivers respond help babies develop emotion-regulation skills as they grow. Responsive regulation does just that—shows babies and toddlers that caregivers are there to meet their needs so that they can feel calm and cared for.

Age Range:	1–2
Skills:	Emotion regulation
Materials:	Varies
Number of Participants:	Baby and caregiver
Where to Play:	Inside or outside

HOW TO PLAY

★ Think of this process in certain categories:
- **Timeliness:** When your baby is upset or dysregulated, respond in a timely manner, as responsiveness is calming and soothing to them. Even if you can't get to your baby right away, responding verbally with a "Hi, baby. I'm here. I'm listening" will help them begin to regulate as they realize they are not alone.
- **Need:** As you learn your baby's specific cries or recognize their needs, helping them regulate becomes much easier. A baby who is hungry won't be soothed for long if they are only given a blanket, and a baby who is tired won't be regulated by the introduction of an interesting new toy. Responding to your baby's specific need will help them regulate more quickly and reduce those upset feelings.
- **Voice:** When babies are upset, communicate with calm, soothing responses. Use a calm voice to assure them that you are there and ready to meet their needs. Calm words, quiet songs, or simple "shh"-ing will communicate to your child that things are okay.
- **Touch:** Gentle physical touches—like back pats, cheek rubs, or cheek-to-cheek contact—are calming and reassuring to babies.
- **Security:** If your child has a security item—such as a blanket or stuffed animal—use this item in your responsive regulation. Touch the blanket to your child's cheek or set the stuffed animal beside them.

* As you provide timely, calm, reassuring regulation to your baby, they will begin to internalize the message that things are safe, and they will be able to use some of these strategies that you use to self-sooth and self-regulate in the future. Some babies will rub their own cheeks or go to their security items when they are upset, because these have become a part of their regulating routine with their beloved caregiver.
* Remember: All babies are unique. What worked for one child might not work for others. And some babies may have higher needs than others and need more time and more responsiveness in order to regulate their emotions. That's okay!

THINKING BACK AND LOOKING AHEAD (FOR CAREGIVERS)

* What did my baby need in this moment?
* How did they respond to my calming strategy?
* What else could I try next time when they are upset?

REGULATING ROUTINES

A consistent routine is a very helpful tool for guiding toddlers to develop self-regulation. A sense of safety and comfort can come from predictable routines and go a long way toward helping your toddler know what to expect.

Age Range:	1–3
Skills:	Emotion regulation
Materials:	Varies
Number of Participants:	Toddler and caregiver
Where to Play:	Inside

HOW TO PLAY

★ Create predictable and consistent routines for your toddler or young child. Routines are like boundaries and help children know what to expect. Here are some examples of routines:
  • Consistent wake-up time
  • Consistent activity schedule: feed/eat, clean up, play, rest
  • Consistent rest times (naps at predictable times)
  • Consistent bedtime routine (bath, stories, song, bed)
★ Remember that while some routines can be child-driven as you notice the needs, preferences, and temperament of your child, some routines will, of course, be parent-driven due to work or commitment schedules. That's okay!
★ Notice what's working for your child. If you notice that your child is dysregulated or upset at a particular time of day, consider if any small changes can be made to the routine to meet the need of the child.
★ Things come up. Routines get interrupted. It's not the end of the world! Just try to get back on schedule when it's possible.

THINKING BACK AND LOOKING AHEAD (FOR CAREGIVERS)

★ How did you feel before we made these routines?
★ How do you feel when you use a routine?
★ Which routine do you like the best, and why?

CALM SPACE

We all need a break sometimes! Create a designated calm space in your home where kids and adults can go when they need a break to relax and regulate their emotions.

Age Range:	1+
Skills:	Emotion regulation
Materials:	Varies, but could include sound machine, noise-canceling headphones, stuffed animals, weighted blanket, coloring book and materials, sequin pillow, journal, etc.
Number of Participants:	Anyone in the family
Where to Play:	Inside or outside

BEFORE YOU START

★ Talk with your family about how this space does not represent a time-out or a punishment for having big feelings. It's an opportunity to take a break from activities that may be upsetting and spend some time doing something soothing so that they can feel calm again and return to what they need to do.

HOW TO PLAY

★ Choose a spot in your house where you can create your calm space. This could be in a corner of a room, in a comfortable chair, or in a quiet nook somewhere.

★ In this space, keep a basket of items that are calming to your child and/or other family members (see Materials list in box).

★ After setting it up, spend time together with your child in the space. Practicing using each of the items. Talk to your child about when they might use each item. For example, they might use the noise-canceling headphones when their brother is practicing his instrument and it's making it hard for them to think.

★ When your child is upset or dysregulated, let them spend some time in the calm space. The first few times they go to the calm space, go with them and provide gentle guidance by suggesting an item or calming activity. Eventually, kids will be able to use the calm space independently.

THINKING BACK AND LOOKING AHEAD

★ How did you feel before you went to the calm space?
★ What activity/item did you use? How did you feel after you used it?
★ How are you feeling now?

NAME THE FEELING

Before kids can regulate their emotions, they need to be able to recognize, understand, and label their emotions. When kids know how they are feeling, they can choose an appropriate strategy for dealing with that feeling.

Age Range:	2+
Skills:	Emotion regulation, communication
Materials:	None
Number of Participants:	Child and caregiver
Where to Play:	Inside, outside, or on video chat

BEFORE YOU START
★ Understand that kids need an "emotional vocabulary" just like they have a vocabulary for other activities. Read books about feelings, talk about feelings, and incorporate feelings into your daily conversations.

HOW TO PLAY
★ Identifying feelings can be practiced anytime, anywhere! Start in "easier" moments when your child is not upset or dysregulated and when you know they are feeling happy, excited, or proud.
★ Ask your child to describe how their body is feeling: "What do you notice about how your body is feeling right now?"
★ Ask your child to name the feeling they are experiencing: "What feeling do you have right now?"
★ When your child has had some practice doing this in moments when they are regulated, give it a try when they are not regulated.
★ Offer praise as they identify the feeling, and reflect it back to them. For example, "You notice that your face is hot and your heart is beating fast. You feel angry. Thanks for telling me how you feel."

THINKING BACK AND LOOKING AHEAD
★ What did you notice about your body?
★ What feeling did you have?
★ When have you felt that way before?
★ What ideas do you have for how you could help yourself feel better?

CONTROLLED BREATHING

Controlled breathing is a great skill for emotion regulation that people of all ages can use anytime and anywhere. In this activity, guide your child's breathing by counting so that all they need to focus on is your voice and their breath.

Age Range:	2+
Skills:	Emotion regulation, self-control, active listening
Materials:	None
Number of Participants:	1+
Where to Play:	Inside, outside, or on video chat

BEFORE YOU START
★ Explain that focusing on our breathing can help us deal with big feelings. Tell children how taking long, slow breaths helps give their brains, lungs, and hearts enough oxygen so that they can work properly.

HOW TO PLAY
★ Practice this controlled-breathing activity when your child is calm so that when they are dysregulated, this practice will come more naturally.
★ Ask your child to sit comfortably, perhaps cross-legged on the floor or in a chair.
★ Ask your child to follow your words and breathe as you guide them, like this:
  • Breathe in for one, two, three, four, five.
  • Breathe out for one, two, three, four, five.
  • Repeat this ten times.
★ When your child is dysregulated, guide them to breathe using this same cuing.

THINKING BACK AND LOOKING AHEAD
★ What was easy about breathing like this?
★ What was hard about breathing like this?
★ How does your body feel after breathing this way?
★ When do you think this might be helpful for you in the future?

BUBBLE BREATHING

This simple exercise can help kids tune in to their breath by taking long, slow, deep breaths. Staying in the present moment in this way can alleviate some of the effects of big feelings so kids can process them. Grab your bubbles and head outside.

Age Range:	2+
Skills:	Emotion regulation
Materials:	Bubbles
Number of Participants:	1+
Where to Play:	Outside

BEFORE YOU START

★ Show your child how to take in a full, deep breath, filling their lungs and belly completely. Practice breathing out slowly.
★ Remind your child that blowing too quickly will not help calm their bodies, and it might instead pop the bubble they are trying to blow.

HOW TO PLAY

★ Hold the bubble wand for your child.
★ Tell them to take in a really big, slow, deep breath, filling their lungs and belly with as much air as possible. Then, tell them to blow it out slowly and completely into the bubble wand, trying to make a big, long bubble.
★ If your child needs help guiding the inhale and exhale for this breath, you can use controlled-breathing cuing:
  • Breathe in for one, two, three, four, five.
  • Blow it out for one, two, three, four, five.
★ Then, tell your child to watch the bubble as it floats away, not taking their eyes off it until it's gone or has popped.
★ Repeat this pattern several times: slow, deep breath in; slow blow out into the bubble wand; and calmly watching the bubble float away.

THINKING BACK AND LOOKING AHEAD

★ How did it feel to take these slow, deep breaths in and blow them out completely?
★ How did you feel while you were watching the bubble float away?

BUDDY BREATHING

Breathing is calming, and doing it with a partner can help kids work together to co-regulate. This practice will help kids tune in to themselves and others to find calm when needed.

Age Range:	2+
Skills:	Emotion regulation, cooperation, self-control
Materials:	None
Number of Participants:	2+ (even numbers)
Where to Play:	Inside or outside

BEFORE YOU START

★ Remind kids that while breathing with a partner, they'll need to pay attention to their partner and move slowly so that everyone can feel safe and calm. Demonstrate what it looks like to breathe in slowly, filling the lungs and belly, and to breathe out slowly, letting all the air out completely.

HOW TO PLAY

★ Each person will need a partner for this activity. Kids and grownups can partner up!
★ Partners will sit cross-legged facing each other.
★ Partners will place their hands together, palms touching, between them.
★ As they breathe in slowly and deeply, partners will slowly move their hands up together.
★ As they breathe out slowly and completely, partners will slowly move their hands down together.
★ During this activity, you can use controlled-breathing cuing:
  • Breathe in and lift hands up for one, two, three, four, five.
  • Breathe out and lower hands for one, two, three, four, five.
★ Repeat this 10–15 times.

THINKING BACK AND LOOKING AHEAD

★ What was easy about breathing like this?
★ What was hard about breathing like this?
★ How does your body feel after breathing this way?
★ What was it like to breathe with a partner?

STUFFED-ANIMAL BREATHING

This focused-breathing practice will help kids visually see the rise and fall of their bellies as they breathe. Get your favorite stuffed animals for this activity.

Age Range:	2+
Skills:	Emotion regulation, self-control
Materials:	Stuffed animals
Number of Participants:	1+
Where to Play:	Inside

BEFORE YOU START

★ Demonstrate what it looks like to breathe in slowly, filling the lungs and belly, and to breathe out slowly, letting all the air out completely.

HOW TO PLAY

★ Kids should lie on their backs. Place a stuffed animal on your child's belly.
★ Kids will practice controlled breathing, watching their stuffed animal rise and fall as they breathe. Remind kids that breathing too quickly will probably make the animal fall! It's important to breathe slowly so the animal stays safe.
★ During this activity, you can use controlled-breathing cuing:
   • Breathe in for one, two, three, four, five.
   • Breathe out for one, two, three, four, five.
★ Repeat this 10–15 times.

THINKING BACK AND LOOKING AHEAD

★ What was easy about breathing like this?
★ What was hard about breathing like this?
★ How does your body feel after breathing this way?

DRAGON BREATHING

Unleash the dragon of your big feelings! Breathing will help calm the body and release tension.

Age Range:	2+
Skills:	Emotion regulation
Materials:	None
Number of Participants:	1+
Where to Play:	Inside or outside

BEFORE YOU START
★ Demonstrate what it looks like to breathe in with three quick breaths, filling the lungs and belly, then to breathe out slowly, letting all the air out completely.

HOW TO PLAY
★ Kids will sit comfortably on the floor or ground for this activity.
★ For this breathing exercise, kids will breathe in with three short inhales and breathe out with one long "Haaaaa!" as if they were fire-breathing dragons.
★ During this activity, you can use the following controlled-breathing cuing:
  • Breathe in quick quick quick.
  • Breathe out HAAAAAAAAA.
★ Repeat this 10–15 times.

THINKING BACK AND LOOKING AHEAD
★ What was easy about breathing like this?
★ What was hard about breathing like this?
★ How does your body feel after breathing this way?

TAP, TAP, SQUEEZE

When big feelings hit, a bit of focused energy, repetition, and sensory pressure can help some kids feel calmer and more regulated. In this activity, kids will practice a simple body-movement pattern that they can use when they have strong feelings.

Age Range:	2+
Skills:	Emotion regulation
Materials:	None
Number of Participants:	1+
Where to Play:	Inside or outside

BEFORE YOU START

★ Explain that this activity might feel different from anything you child has done before. Sometimes, different can feel uncomfortable. Encourage your child to give it a try even though it's different.

★ Remind your child to move slowly through the pattern. Let them know that saying the pattern aloud while they do it might be helpful and calming too.

HOW TO PLAY

★ Practice this strategy when your child is calm so that when they have big feelings, it comes more easily.

★ Guide your child to tap their left hand on their right shoulder, tap their right hand on their left shoulder, then squeeze themselves in a hug. Release.

★ Continue in this pattern. Tap, tap, squeeze, release. Repeat this 10–15 times.

THINKING BACK AND LOOKING AHEAD

★ How did you feel while you did this activity?

★ How does your body feel now?

★ When do you think you might use this strategy in the future?

ENERGY RELEASE

Big feelings come with big energy. Practice safe ways to release that energy in this activity using easy exercises that kids can do almost anywhere.

Age Range:	2+
Skills:	Emotion regulation, self-control
Materials:	None
Number of Participants:	1+
Where to Play:	Inside or outside

BEFORE YOU START

★ Explain that sometimes when we have big feelings, our bodies feel like they have lots of energy or tension inside. Sometimes that energy might feel like it's going to explode out of our bodies! If we can let some of that energy out in slow, controlled ways, we can keep ourselves and other people safe.

★ Show your child how to safely do each exercise.

HOW TO PLAY

★ To practice releasing energy or tension, lead your child through the following exercises. Do 10–20 repetitions of each, depending on your child's age and comfort level:
  • Wall push-ups
  • Calf raises
  • Palm presses
  • Squats
  • Hopping in place or jumping jacks

THINKING BACK AND LOOKING AHEAD

★ Which of these exercises did you enjoy most?
★ How did your body feel while we did the activity?
★ How does your body feel now?
★ When do you think you might use this energy-release activity to manage your feelings in a safe way?

REST STOP

For some kids, stopping and calming their bodies is no easy feat! This activity will help kids practice regulating their emotions by first raising their heart rates and then learning how to slow them, calming their bodies and minds.

Age Range:	2+
Skills:	Emotion regulation, self-control
Materials:	None
Number of Participants:	1+
Where to Play:	Outside

BEFORE YOU START

★ Explain that sometimes when we have strong emotions like fear, anger, or worry, our hearts might feel like they are pumping extra hard, just like they do when we exercise. Being able to calm our hearts will help us think more clearly and make good choices when we have those big feelings.

HOW TO PLAY

★ Players will spread out in their own personal space.
★ The adult leader will call out, "Hit the highway!" Players can run freely in the space. Let players run for thirty or more seconds to get their heart rates up.
★ When the adult leader calls out, "Rest stop!" players will freeze where they are, sit down, and practice controlled breathing for sixty seconds. During this portion, you can use controlled-breathing cuing:
  • Breathe in for one, two, three, four, five.
  • Breathe out for one, two, three, four, five.
★ After this, call out, "Hit the highway!" again to repeat the activity.

THINKING BACK AND LOOKING AHEAD

★ How did your body feel when you were on the highway?
★ How did your body feel when you were at the rest stop?

BODY SCAN

Emotion regulation requires kids to tune in to their bodies and recognize what's going on inside. When they can notice what's happening inside their bodies as they experience certain feelings, they can choose appropriate calming strategies to try. In this activity, kids will practice noticing what's happening in their bodies, one area at a time.

Age Range:	4+
Skills:	Emotion regulation, self-control
Materials:	None
Number of Participants:	1+
Where to Play:	Inside or outside

BEFORE YOU START

★ Explain that this activity might feel different from anything your child has done before. Sometimes, different can feel uncomfortable. Encourage your child to give it a try even though it's different and to let you know if they feel uncomfortable.

HOW TO PLAY

★ Ask kids to sit comfortably.
★ For this activity, kids may close their eyes if they are comfortable doing so, but it's okay if they'd like to keep their eyes open.
★ Guide kids through the body scan using the following cuing:
  • Let's practice noticing what's happening in your body. We'll focus on one part of your body at a time. Just notice what's happening in that part of your body. Is it tense? Is it tight? Is it warm? Does it feel tingly? Just notice.
  • Let start with your toes. Focus your mind on your toes. What do you notice? (Pause for 20–30 seconds to give kids time to notice, either silently or aloud.)
  • Let's move to your legs. Focus your mind on your legs. What do you notice? (Pause for 20–30 seconds to give kids time to notice.)
  • Let's move to your belly. Focus your mind on your belly. What do you notice? (Pause for 20–30 seconds to give kids time to notice.)

(continued on next page)

- Let's move to your back. Focus your mind on your back. What do you notice? (Pause for 20–30 seconds to give kids time to notice.)
- Let's move to your chest. Focus your mind on your chest. What do you notice? (Pause for 20–30 seconds to give kids time to notice.)
- Let's move to your fingers. Focus your mind on your fingers. What do you notice? (Pause for 20–30 seconds to give kids time to notice.)
- Let's move to your arms. Focus your mind on your arms. What do you notice? (Pause for 20–30 seconds to give kids time to notice.)
- Let's move to your shoulders. Focus your mind on your shoulders. What do you notice? (Pause for 20–30 seconds to give kids time to notice.)
- Let's move to your neck. Focus your mind on your neck. What do you notice? (Pause for 20–30 seconds to give kids time to notice.)
- Last, let's move to your head. Focus your mind on your head. What do you notice? (Pause for 20–30 seconds to give kids time to notice.)

THINKING BACK AND LOOKING AHEAD

★ How did you feel while we did this activity?
★ What did you notice in your toes? Legs? Belly? Back? Chest? Fingers? Arms? Shoulders? Neck? Head?
★ Did any part of your body feel tense or tight?
★ Did any part of your body feel tingly?
★ Did any part of your body feel calm?

PROGRESSIVE MUSCLE RELAXATION

Releasing tension from the body is a great emotion-regulation strategy than can be employed anywhere and anytime without any tools. When kids feel strong emotions, like anger or frustration, they might notice tension in their bodies. This practice will help them release that tension in a safe way so that they can feel more calm and in control.

Age Range:	4+
Skills:	Emotion regulation, self-control
Materials:	None
Number of Participants:	1+
Where to Play:	Inside or outside

BEFORE YOU START

★ Explain that this activity might feel different from anything your child has done before. Sometimes, different can feel uncomfortable. Encourage your child to give it a try even though it's different and to let you know if they feel uncomfortable.

★ Remind kids that they should squeeze but not to the point that they're hurting.

HOW TO PLAY

★ Ask kids to sit comfortably. They may close their eyes if they are comfortable doing so, but it's okay if they'd like to keep their eyes open.

★ Guide kids through the progressive muscle relaxation using the following cuing:
  • Let's practice letting go of tension in our bodies. We'll focus on one part of our bodies at a time. We'll squeeze that part of our bodies and then let go.
  • Let's start with our faces. Squeeze your face as tight as you can and hold for one, two, three, four, five (older kids will be able to do this for ten seconds). Release. Shake it gently.
  • Let's move to your shoulders. Lift your shoulders toward your ears and gently squeeze and hold for one, two, three, four, five. Release. Shake them gently.

(continued on next page)

- Let's move to your arms (biceps). Squeeze your arms as tight as you can and hold for one, two, three, four, five. Release. Shake them gently.
- Let's move to your hands. Squeeze your hands as tight as you can into fists and hold for one, two, three, four, five. Release. Shake them gently.
- Let's move to your belly. Squeeze your belly muscles as tight as you can and hold for one, two, three, four, five. Release. Shake gently.
- Let's move to your bottom. Squeeze your bottom muscles as tight as you can and hold for one, two, three, four, five. Release. Shake gently.
- Let's move to your upper legs (quadriceps). Squeeze your legs as tight as you can and hold for one, two, three, four, five. Release. Shake them gently.
- Last, let's move to your toes. Squeeze your toes as tight as you can and hold for one, two, three, four, five. Release. Shake them gently.
- Give your whole body a few gentle shakes.

THINKING BACK AND LOOKING AHEAD

★ What did you notice while we did this activity?
★ How are you feeling after doing this activity?
★ Does your body feel tense and tight now or loose and relaxed?
★ When do you think doing this activity would be helpful for you?

Progressive muscle relaxation is an evidence-based strategy to use for calming the body in times of dysregulation. When doing this with kids, remind them that when they squeeze their muscles, they should feel tightness but not pain! If they are feeling pain, they should loosen their squeeze. Put focus on large muscles of the legs in this activity so as not to give anyone a muscle spasm in the calf (a charley horse—ouch!).

KITE, TREE, FROG

For young kids, a big part of emotion regulation is body control. Emotions can come out as behaviors, so learning to control their bodies can help kids process their big emotions. In this activity, kids will practice getting into three controlled yoga poses from active movements to simulate calming from big feelings.

Age Range:	4+
Skills:	Emotion regulation, self-control, active listening
Materials:	None
Number of Participants:	1+
Where to Play:	Inside or outside

BEFORE YOU START

★ Show kids how to do each yoga pose safely. Remind kids that it's important to be in control of their bodies while in these poses so that they do not get hurt.

★ **Kite pose:** Plant your feet firmly on the ground. Press your palms together overhead. Gently lean to one side like a kite floating in the wind.

★ **Beginner tree pose:** Plant your feet firmly on the ground. Lift one foot and place it on the inside of the other ankle. Bring your palms together in front of your heart or overhead.

★ **Frog pose:** Plant your feet firmly on the ground, wider than hip-width apart. Bring your palms together in front of your heart. Gently squat down, bending the knees. For safety, make sure the knees do not extend past the toes.

HOW TO PLAY

★ Players will stand in their own personal space so that they cannot touch others.

★ Players will hop in place until the adult leader calls out a yoga pose. Poses include kite pose, tree pose, and frog pose (instructions for these poses are in the Before You Start section).

★ When the adult leader calls out the name of a pose, kids will get into the pose and hold it until the adult leader tells them to hop again. While in the pose, kids can take slow, deep breaths as they hold it and wait for the next instruction. The adult leader could also ask them to move from one yoga pose to another instead of going back to hopping.

(continued on next page)

★ Continue playing for 5–10 minutes depending on the age and engagement of the kids.

THINKING BACK AND LOOKING AHEAD

★ How did your body feel while you were hopping?
★ How did your body feel while you were in the poses?
★ Which pose was easiest for you?
★ Which pose was hardest for you?
★ When do you think you could use these poses in the future to help yourself feel calm?

MINDFUL MEDITATION

Mindfulness, or bringing attention and awareness to the present moment, is a powerful tool for emotion regulation. Practicing mindfulness can help kids interrupt thoughts of the past or future and instead tune in to their bodies and experiences in the present moment. In this activity, you'll lead a mindful meditation with your child using the script given or your favorite mindfulness app.

Age Range:	4+
Skills:	Emotion regulation
Materials:	Sound machine (optional)
Number of Participants:	1+
Where to Play:	Inside or outside

BEFORE YOU START
★ Explain what mindfulness is and how it can help kids feel in control.

HOW TO PLAY
★ Sit comfortably in a quiet space with as few distractions as possible.
★ Read the following mindfulness script or choose a meditation from your favorite mindfulness app or online resource. For younger children, ages 4–6, choose a meditation that is under two minutes. Older children may be able to do up to five minutes with practice.

Mindfulness Script for Ages 4–6:
Today, we are going to try a mindfulness exercise. This means that we're going to focus our minds on what we're doing right now. Just listen to my voice, and I'll tell you what to think about in your mind.

A turtle likes to go into a safe place to calm his body and mind. We're going to imagine our own safe places today. To prepare, let's begin to control our breathing. Let's inhale...and exhale. Inhale...and exhale. Take one more deep breath in and slowly let it go.

(continued on next page)

Now, let's close our eyes and push away our thoughts. Let your thoughts float away like a leaf in the breeze. Watch your thoughts float away in your mind.

A turtle goes inside his shell to relax. In his shell, he is protected from the world. As you sit with your eyes closed, imagine you are in a shell. Picture your shell all around you. Notice what your shell looks like. Imagine how it would feel if you reached out and touched it.

While you are inside your shell, push out all your other thoughts as they sneak in. Think only about how you are safe in your shell. Let your worries roll down your back one at a time. Let the stress of the world slide off your back. You are in your peaceful, calm place. Enjoy your peaceful, calm place for a moment.

Take a deep breath in through your nose and slowly blow it out of your mouth. Breathe in through your nose and slowly out through your mouth. Open your eyes as you come out from your safe shell.

THINKING BACK AND LOOKING AHEAD

★ How were you feeling inside your shell?
★ What did your shell look like?
★ How are you feeling now that you are outside your shell?
★ When might it be helpful for you to imagine that you are in your peaceful, safe shell?

Mindfulness Script for Ages 7+:
Today, we will try a mindfulness activity. We will focus on things that bring us joy and notice how this affects our bodies and minds. To prepare, let's sit comfortably, close our eyes, and inhale...and exhale. Inhale...and exhale. Take one more deep breath in and slowly release it.

As you sit comfortably in your space, close your eyes and push away all other thoughts. Allow the thoughts to float away, leaving space in your mind for our activity today.

Now, as you sit with your eyes closed, think about what joy means to you. In your mind, create your own personal picture of joy. What does joy look like? How does joy feel? How do you know when you are feeling joyful?

As you focus on these questions, what things or people enter your mind? What things or people in your life bring you joy? What experiences have you had in which joy was the feeling that flowed through your body and mind?

While you think of these people, things, or experiences, notice how your body feels. Where in your body do you feel joy? What sensations do you experience? Allow yourself to sink into that joy. Let it cover your body in warmth.

★ Now, in your mind, complete this sentence: "I express and embrace the joy that _____ gives me." Notice how it feels in your body to actually express your joy.

THINKING BACK AND LOOKING AHEAD

★ What does joy mean to you?
★ What does joy feel like in your body?
★ What people, things, or experiences did you think of when focusing on joy?
★ How often do you express your joy? What was it like to do so today?
★ How do you think making an effort to express joy could positively impact your life and the community?

....

If you're looking for some apps and resources to use for kid-friendly mindful meditations, check out these great resources: Headspace app (Meditation for Kids feature); Stop, Breathe & Think app; Smiling Mind app; Sleep Meditations for Kids app; and *Cosmic Kids Yoga* on *YouTube*.

....

CREATE YOUR OWN MANTRAS

Mantras are words or phrases that help us feel calm, powerful, and in control of our bodies and minds. In this activity, kids will create their own mindful mantra or calming phrase that they can repeat to themselves when they have strong emotions or need time to regulate.

Age Range:	4+
Skills:	Emotion regulation
Materials:	Paper and coloring utensils (optional)
Number of Participants:	1+
Where to Play:	Inside or outside

BEFORE YOU START

★ Explain that sometimes when we have big feelings, repeating a word or phrase to ourselves can help us feel calmer. Give your child an example of a mantra that you could repeat to yourself when you feel upset or worried, like, "Just breathe. Just breathe. Just breathe."

HOW TO PLAY

★ Make a list of calming words or phrases together with your child.
★ Let your child pick the word or phrase that they like best and think will help them feel calm.
★ Practice calmly repeating the mantra.
★ Your child may also benefit from visualizing an image as they repeat the mantra. For example, if their mantra is "I can breathe," they might picture in their mind a balloon being inflated.
★ If desired, let your child write the mantra on paper and draw a picture to accompany it as a reminder they can look at when they need to use their mantra.
★ Practice calmly repeating the mantra again with the mental image your child came up with to accompany the mantra.
★ When your child has strong emotions, remind them to use their mantra.

THINKING BACK AND LOOKING AHEAD

★ Why did you choose this phrase/word for your mantra?
★ How do you feel as you repeat this to yourself?
★ When do you think you will use this mantra?

SENSORY GROUNDING

Sometimes when kids have big emotions, their thoughts are focused on past events or future possibilities, or they might find themselves unable to focus at all. Grounding techniques are strategies to help kids reconnect with what's happening right now in the moment.

Age Range:	4+
Skills:	Emotion regulation
Materials:	None
Number of Participants:	1+
Where to Play:	Inside or outside

BEFORE YOU START

★ Explain that this activity might feel different than anything your child has done before. Sometimes, different can feel uncomfortable. Encourage your child to give it a try even though it's different.

HOW TO PLAY

★ Practice this grounding strategy when your child is calm so that when they have big feelings, it comes more easily.
★ Guide your child to use their senses in the following way:
  • Notice and name five things you see right now.
  • Notice and name four things you hear right now.
  • Notice and name three things you can touch right now.
  • Notice and name two things you can smell right now.
  • Notice and name one thing you can taste right now.
★ If your child is quick to say "I don't know" or "I don't smell anything," resist the urge to move on to the next sense. Give them time, and encourage them to just take a moment to notice.
★ When your child has strong feelings and is unable to talk or process the event or emotion, guide them through this grounding technique to help them reconnect to the present moment and calm their body and mind.

(continued on next page)

THINKING BACK AND LOOKING AHEAD

★ How did you feel while you were doing this activity?

★ Do you think you would normally notice the things you noticed with your senses today?

★ When do you think this activity might be helpful for you in the future?

If your child is having trouble identifying things in the environment using their senses, try this more concrete grounding exercise instead:

• Name five colors you see in the environment.

• Name four shapes you see.

• Name three soft things you see.

• Name two people you see.

• Name one book you see.

Swap out any of these things with something else concrete in your environment. The whole idea of grounding is that kids reconnect with what is real in their environment and move away from spiraling toward thoughts of the past or worries about the future!

LET IT GO

Sometimes, hard things happen, and it's difficult to accept them and move on. In this activity, kids will practice letting go of events or experiences that led to their big feelings so they can move on with their day.

Age Range:	4+
Skills:	Emotion regulation
Materials:	Paper, pencils or markers
Number of Participants:	1+
Where to Play:	Inside

BEFORE YOU START

★ Remind kids that sometimes we go through hard or frustrating things that leave us feeling angry, sad, or worried. It's okay to feel these things! But if we're having a hard time moving on from what happened, we can try something to help ourselves let it go.

HOW TO PLAY

★ Practice this strategy when your child is calm so that when they have big feelings, it comes more easily.
★ Ask your child to write about or draw a picture of a difficult experience they went through recently that was hard to move on from. Talk about the event, how they felt, and how they're feeling now.
★ Once the child has drawn a picture, they can decide how to "officially" let go from one of these options:
  • Fold the paper they wrote or drew on into a paper airplane. Send it flying into a recycling bin and say, "I'm letting go of this so I can fly on with my day!"
  • Stand over the recycling bin. Tear the paper into smaller shreds and drop them in. Say, "I'm letting go of all the little pieces of this so I can move on!"
  • Fill a bowl with water. Place the paper in the water and watch the words or colors melt away. Say, "I'm letting this melt away so I can move on with my day!"

THINKING BACK AND LOOKING AHEAD

★ What was it like to write about or draw about the experience?
★ How did you feel when you let go of your paper in some way?
★ How are you feeling now?

CHAPTER 10

THINKING CAP ON! PROBLEM-SOLVING SKILLS

WHAT IS PROBLEM-SOLVING?

Problem-solving is a skill used to approach new and challenging tasks or to overcome unfamiliar obstacles. Specific problem-solving skills include thinking creatively, trying new strategies, learning from mistakes, and taking risks.

WHAT DOES PROBLEM-SOLVING LOOK AND SOUND LIKE?

Problem-solving can take on many different forms, actions, and words. Some examples of what problem-solving looks and sounds like include:

* Trying new things
* Narrowing down a list of ideas
* Using mistakes to generate new ideas
* Throwing away first attempts that don't work
* Asking questions
* Expressing frustration

PROBLEM-SOLVING IN KID-FRIENDLY TERMS

To explain problem-solving to your kid, try saying something like this:

Every day we face tasks or challenges that we've never faced before. When we try new things, they might be hard, or we might not know how to do them, and that's okay. That's how we learn new things! We can be problem-solvers by trying multiple strategies, learning from our mistakes, looking at the problem in a new way, listening to ideas from other people, and asking questions.

WHY PROBLEM-SOLVING SKILLS ARE IMPORTANT

As kids are exposed to new tasks, challenges, and experiences, they'll have opportunities for engaging in problem-solving. Part of growing as a learner and an individual is trying new things and solving new problems.

One of the most important skills that comes out of problem-solving opportunities is frustration tolerance. As kids make mistakes and experience failure in these new tasks and challenges, they will experience frustration. Being able to work with this frustration and use it as a motivating factor instead of a limiting factor will propel kids toward success and encourage them to be flexible thinkers who persevere.

WHERE AND WHEN KIDS WILL USE PROBLEM-SOLVING SKILLS

Opportunities for problem-solving will present themselves in the classroom, on the playground, at home, and eventually in the workplace. In the classroom, kids will be faced with new information and tasks and asked to synthesize their learning in new ways that require problem-solving skills. On the playground, kids will undoubtedly find themselves needing to problem-solve with peers to play in a way that includes everyone or in a way that's fun for everyone.

In order to learn to be problem-solvers, kids need lots of opportunities for failure and mistakes. As kids face struggles in their efforts, they will also learn to try new strategies, be flexible, use analytical thinking, be persistent, and practice decision-making skills.

LOOKING AHEAD

In this chapter, you'll find activities to help kids practice these important skills. Dive into STEM challenges, play games that require flexible thinking, and try activities that require design, modification, and analytical thinking for success. As you complete these activities, monitor your child's frustration levels and encourage them to use calming strategies such as deep breathing if they feel tempted to give up. Model problem-solving for them by wondering aloud how they might change their strategy or try something new to achieve their goal.

MISSING ITEM

Ticktock, ticktock! Grab a clock and a blanket for this problem-solving activity with your baby or toddler. After you cover the clock, your baby will have a chance to practice problem-solving by listening for the ticktock sound and pulling the blanket off the clock. For an older baby, place a small item under one of three cups and let your baby use problem-solving skills to find it.

Age Range:	1–2
Skills:	Problem-solving
Materials:	Ticking clock or ticking timer, blanket; or for older babies, 1 small (non-choking-hazard-size) toy, 3 cups
Number of Participants:	Baby and caregiver
Where to Play:	Inside

HOW TO PLAY WITH A YOUNGER BABY

* Show your baby the clock.
* Mimic the ticktock sound of the clock for a few minutes with your baby.
* Let your baby touch and hold the clock (if it is plastic).
* Then, place a blanket over the clock. Ask your baby, "Where did it go? Where is the ticktock clock?"
* Let your baby search for the clock and pull the blanket away.

HOW TO PLAY WITH AN OLDER BABY

* Show your baby a small toy that they cannot choke on. Talk about what the item is. Describe the toy to your baby. Let your baby touch or hold the item.
* Line up the cups in front of your baby. Place the toy under one of the cups.
* Let your baby search for the item under the cups.

THINKING BACK AND LOOKING AHEAD

* Celebrate your baby's success! "You found the ticktock clock!"
* Do the activity again, but move the covered clock farther away to encourage your baby to crawl to it.
* If you are using the cups, do the activity again, but place the item under a different cup this time!

PUSH IT

What does that button do?! Give your baby a toy that has buttons to push or levers to pull, resulting in opening or popping up. Let your child explore the buttons to develop early problem-solving thinking.

Age Range:	1–2
Skills:	Problem-solving
Materials:	Toy with buttons to push or levers to pull resulting in opening or popping up
Number of Participants:	Baby and caregiver
Where to Play:	Inside

HOW TO PLAY

★ Give your child the toy and let them explore. See what happens as they look at the item and reach for the buttons.

★ If your child spends more than a few minutes looking at the toy without pushing any of the buttons, push a button for them to demonstrate what happens. Celebrate what happened: "We made the door open!" or "We made the bird come out!"

★ Then, give the toy back and encourage your child to press the other buttons on the toy to see what happens. If they succeed, celebrate their success.

THINKING BACK AND LOOKING AHEAD (FOR CAREGIVERS)

★ Think back and recall if there were certain types of buttons that your baby opened easily or had difficulty opening.

★ Think back and recall which button your baby really seemed to enjoy the most.

FRIENDLY FORT

Building a fort is a timeless activity for kids of all ages. Grab some household or outdoor supplies and let kids build a free-standing fort. They'll need to problem-solve and try new strategies to make sure the fort stands on its own.

Age Range:	3+
Skills:	Problem-solving
Materials:	Household items such as chairs and sheets for an indoor fort, or pool noodles, a tarp, and lawn chairs for an outdoor fort; timer (optional)
Number of Participants:	1+
Where to Play:	Inside or outside

BEFORE YOU START

★ Let players share some ideas about how they might complete the task.

HOW TO PLAY

★ Challenge players to build a fort that stands on its own with the supplies that you provide them.
★ The fort should be big enough for all players to fit inside.
★ You may choose to set a timer for an added layer of difficulty.

THINKING BACK AND LOOKING AHEAD

★ What was difficult about this activity?
★ What was fun about it?
★ Did any part of your fort fall or not work out how you expected? How did you handle this?
★ What would you do differently if you built another fort?

THE FLOOR IS LAVA

Keep those feet off the floor, because the floor is lava! In this problem-solving activity, kids will construct a safe path from one side of the room to the other so that they can travel across it without touching their feet to the ground. They'll have to use their cooperation skills as they build a path and revise their strategies if their feet touch the lava.

Age Range:	3+
Skills:	Problem-solving, cooperation
Materials:	Household items such as pillows, stools, laundry basket, etc.
Number of Participants:	2+
Where to Play:	Inside

BEFORE YOU START
★ Review the rules and talk about how to use the household items safely.
★ Give players time to plan how they will design their path.

HOW TO PLAY
★ In this game, players' feet should not touch the floor. Players will use the household items you provide to make a path from one side of the room to the other.
★ When players have finished their path, try it out!
★ If anyone's feet touch the floor, start over at the beginning.
★ If players are having trouble getting across after multiple attempts, give them time to modify their design.
★ When players are successful, remove one or two of the household items used in the path and let them redesign it.

THINKING BACK AND LOOKING AHEAD
★ How did it feel when your foot touched the lava and you had to start over?
★ How did you work together to plan your path?
★ What would you do differently next time?

MAKE YOUR OWN GAME

Game on! Grab some items from around the house and challenge kids to create their own game. They'll plan the rules, the points system, and all things that go into games. Kids will need to use flexible thinking to use the items in new ways and problem-solving to plan the game. Bonus: This is a great opportunity to practice good sportsmanship too!

Age Range:	4+
Skills:	Problem-solving, flexible thinking, good sportsmanship
Materials:	Tennis balls, Frisbees, sand buckets, cones, or other random items; paper and pencil (optional)
Number of Participants:	2+
Where to Play:	Inside or outside

BEFORE YOU START

* Set ground rules for how items can be used safely (like no throwing balls over-hand in the house!).
* Review what it means to be a good sport. A good sport is playing to have fun, not just playing to win. Good sports also encourage everyone, not just themselves or their own team. At the end of the game, good sports congratulate the winner if they lose. And if they win, it's okay to celebrate a bit but not too much or in a way that might hurt someone's feelings. Finally, good sports say, "Good game!" no matter who wins or loses.

HOW TO PLAY

* In this activity, players will use the materials you provide to make up their own game. You can set a rule that all materials must be used or that the players can choose two or three of the items you provide. It's up to you!

* Children may need extra support and guidance in this activity. Ask them questions like:
  * How will the game start?
  * Who goes first?
  * How do you score a point?
  * What can you do?
  * What can you not do?
  * What will you use this item for?
  * How will you know your turn is over?
  * When does the game end?
  * How will you know who wins?
* Players may write the rules on paper or simply share them aloud.
* When the game has been designed, play the game together!

THINKING BACK AND LOOKING AHEAD
* Did you base your game on another game you've played?
* Did you forget to include a rule in your game that you realized you needed once you started playing?
* Who was a good sport in the game?
* How did they show good sportsmanship?
* What would you do differently next time?

INVENTION CONVENTION

Grab some craft supplies or unwanted items from around the house and challenge kids to build a new toy that they think others would like to play with. Kids will need to use flexible thinking and creativity to see these craft and household items in new ways!

Age Range:	4+
Skills:	Problem-solving, flexible thinking
Materials:	Paper straws, yarn, tape, craft sticks, empty paper towel rolls, paper clips, sticky notes, glue, or other odd items that can be used for crafts; paper and pencil (optional)
Number of Participants:	1+
Where to Play:	Inside or outside

BEFORE YOU START

★ Give kids time to brainstorm!
★ You may want to offer guided support with this process. This might sound like:
  • What kind of toy would you like to have that you've never seen before? A space toy? A vehicle? A kitchen toy?
  • Which of these supplies do you think you can use?
  • How might you use this material in your design?

HOW TO PLAY

★ Give children some of the supplies listed or your own household or craft supplies.
★ If you have multiple children doing the activity, they can work together for a cooperative activity to encourage communication and cooperation, or they can work independently.
★ The object of this activity is for kids to use the supplies provided to build a new toy that they think other kids would like to play with. Encourage kids to draw a design on paper first before they start building.
★ Younger children might need support or help with holding materials while gluing, but let them take the lead.

* When they are finished, give them time to explain what their toy is and how kids can play with it!
* If the children worked independently, they can trade toys and play with one another's designs.

THINKING BACK AND LOOKING AHEAD

* What struggles did you have while you were building? How did you overcome these struggles?
* How is your design different from your original idea?
* What changes did you make?

BALANCING ACT

Getting kids to balance toys on a homemade seesaw will encourage them to use problem-solving skills to create balance and try new strategies when things don't work out!

Age Range:	4+
Skills:	Problem-solving
Materials:	Materials to create a small tabletop seesaw (like a triangular block and a small wooden plank or ruler), 8–10 toys of different sizes and weights
Number of Participants:	1+
Where to Play:	Inside or outside

BEFORE YOU START

★ Let players share some ideas about how they might complete the task.

HOW TO PLAY

★ Create a small seesaw that will sit on a tabletop or on the ground, using a triangular block and a wooden board or other supplies that you have on hand. The goal of this activity is for the children to balance the toys on the seesaw.
★ Let the kids place the toys on the seesaw, correcting for imbalances on their own.
★ After they get the toys balanced, you may choose to add more toys or remove just one for an added challenge.

THINKING BACK AND LOOKING AHEAD

★ What struggles did you have while trying to balance the seesaw? How did you overcome these struggles?
★ How did you figure out which toys should go on each side?
★ Did you find a strategy for making small changes to find the balance?

PAPER AIRPLANE

This simple activity packs a problem-solving punch! Make paper airplanes and set a goal for how far they will fly. Kids will have to test their designs, then revise them, all the while using problem-solving skills to learn from failed attempts. Practicing determination and resiliency will serve them well in all areas of life.

Age Range:	4+
Skills:	Problem-solving
Materials:	Paper
Number of Participants:	1+
Where to Play:	Inside or outside

BEFORE YOU START
* Look over some paper airplane designs online.

HOW TO PLAY
* Players will make paper airplanes in the activity.
* Set a starting point and finish line. The goal is for the airplanes to fly from the start to the finish line.
* Give players time to design their paper airplanes.
* When players are ready, they will stand at the starting point and throw the paper airplanes. You may choose to give each player 1–3 tries.
* Give players time to modify their designs or create new paper airplanes and try again!

THINKING BACK AND LOOKING AHEAD
* How did it feel if your plane didn't reach the finish line?
* What strategies did you try to make your plane the best it could be?
* What would you do differently next time?

SPAGHETTI SKYSCRAPER

This STEM challenge will give kids a chance to practice their design, redesign, flexible-thinking, and problem-solving skills as they build a tower with uncooked spaghetti.

Age Range:	4+
Skills:	Problem-solving, flexible thinking
Materials:	Uncooked spaghetti, painter's tape
Number of Participants:	1+
Where to Play:	Inside or outside

BEFORE YOU START
★ Let players share some ideas about how they might complete the task.
★ Talk about what they can do if they feel frustrated during the activity: take deep breaths, encourage each other, or try new strategies.

HOW TO PLAY
★ Players will build a skyscraper that stands on its own using only uncooked spaghetti and 1 foot of painter's tape.
★ Give players their materials. If there is more than one player, they can work together to make it a cooperative activity.
★ For added difficulty, you may choose to set a goal for how tall the skyscraper will be (2 feet, 3 feet, or more!) and/or a time limit.

THINKING BACK AND LOOKING AHEAD
★ How did you feel if your spaghetti noodles broke?
★ How did you feel if your tower fell?
★ How did you handle your frustration?
★ What strategies did you try that didn't work?
★ What strategies did you try that did work? How did you feel when your strategies worked?
★ What would you do differently next time?

FLEXIBLE DRAWING

In this activity, kids will begin a drawing, pass it to a friend, and then continue someone else's drawing. They'll have to think flexibly and bring their teamwork attitude!

Age Range:	4+
Skills:	Problem-solving, flexible thinking, cooperation
Materials:	Paper, crayons, timer
Number of Participants:	2+
Where to Play:	Inside or outside

BEFORE YOU START

★ Talk about what it means to be flexible. Children will start a drawing, but someone else will add to it. The final drawing might not look exactly like what the initial artist envisioned. And that's okay! We'll all end up with special drawings.

HOW TO PLAY

★ Give each child paper and crayons.
★ Each child will begin drawing anything they want. Set a timer for 1–2 minutes.
★ When the timer goes off, each child will pass their drawing to another child.
★ Each child will continue the drawing they have been given for another 1–2 minutes. They should not ask what the drawing is intended to be.
★ Continue setting the timer and passing drawings among the children until the drawings are done (when every child has added to each drawing).
★ Return each drawing to its original artist.

THINKING BACK AND LOOKING AHEAD

★ Does your drawing look like what you planned?
★ What is something you like that someone added to your drawing?
★ How do you think working together made our drawings special and unique?

If your child is alone for this activity, it can be completed independently too. Simply get a piece of paper and start a drawing with a shape, squiggly line, or something else, then ask your child to turn it into their very own masterpiece.

ANIMAL TRANSPORT

In this activity, kids will build a transportation device to carry a stuffed animal from one side of the room to the other. They'll have to build and modify their design after testing it to see what works. This activity will help kids learn from mistakes and practice flexible thinking.

Age Range:	5+
Skills:	Problem-solving, flexible thinking
Materials:	Craft materials (e.g., paper straws, yarn, tape, craft sticks, paper clips, sticky notes, etc.), stuffed animal
Number of Participants:	1+
Where to Play:	Inside or outside

BEFORE YOU START

★ Let players share some ideas about how they might complete the task.

HOW TO PLAY

★ Give players the craft materials for the activity as well as the stuffed animal.
★ Players will use the materials provided to make something to transport the stuffed animal from one side of the room to the other. When transporting the stuffed animal, players should not be touching the stuffed animal at all and should only have hands on the materials used for the transportation device.
★ Give players time to construct and test their design. They can modify the design as needed after test runs.
★ When players are ready, transport the animal.

THINKING BACK AND LOOKING AHEAD

★ How did you feel when your stuffed animal fell out of the test designs?
★ How did you handle your frustration?
★ What strategies did you try that didn't work?
★ What strategies did you try that did work? How did you feel when your strategies worked?
★ What would you do differently next time?

INFOMERCIAL

During this game, kids will create an infomercial to sell a product. The product will be a common item, and they'll come up with a new use for this item. Being able to think flexibly will help kids develop problem-solving skills they can use in a variety of situations.

Age Range:	5+
Skills:	Problem-solving, flexible thinking, cooperation
Materials:	A variety of household items (e.g., a Frisbee, a mop, a whisk)
Number of Participants:	1+
Where to Play:	Inside, outside, or on video chat

BEFORE YOU START
★ Remind your child that thinking flexibly means we think outside the box. Frame it as an opportunity to show off their amazing ideas and creativity! Give your child an example of a time when you used an item for a purpose other than how it was intended (like that time you used sugar packets to level a wobbly table!). If your child is unfamiliar with infomercials, find some video clips online to show them so they really know how to sell their product!

HOW TO PLAY
★ Give the participants a household item. They will create an infomercial skit to sell this item to you...but there's a twist! They must create a new use for this item that is totally separate from its intended use.
★ Give the kids some time to talk over their ideas and prepare their skit.
★ Have them perform the infomercial skit for you or the whole family!

THINKING BACK AND LOOKING AHEAD
★ What did you enjoy about this activity?
★ What was hard about this activity?
★ Did you get stuck at any point? How did you get past it?
★ How can thinking outside the box help you in other situations?
★ Tell me about a time when thinking outside the box was hard for you.

CREATIVE STORYTELLING

In this game, kids will write a story or create a skit about a character using adjective and career cards. Some of the adjective-and-career combinations might feel silly, so kids will need to bring their creativity and problem-solving skills to complete the activity.

Age Range:	5+
Skills:	Problem-solving, flexible thinking
Materials:	Notecards or strips of paper, pencil or marker, timer (optional)
Number of Participants:	1+
Where to Play:	Inside, outside, or on video chat

BEFORE YOU START

★ Review all the adjectives to make sure that players know what they mean, and review the careers to make sure players know what they are.

HOW TO PLAY

★ On notecards or strips of paper, write a variety of adjectives and careers. Here are some suggestions:

Adjectives		Careers	
Silly	Grouchy	Shortstop	Quarterback
Sleepy	Confused	Pastry chef	Math teacher
Funny	Nervous	App designer	Illustrator
Greedy	Thoughtful	*YouTube* star	Dog trainer
Lucky	Strong	Pediatrician	Principal
Jolly	Clever	Podcaster	Racecar driver
Hungry	Dizzy	Author	Movie director

* At random, draw one adjective card and one career card.
* Players will then make up a story or a skit about a person with the career and adjective cards they have drawn.
* You may wish to set a timer for an added level of difficulty.
* At the end of the time, players will tell their story or perform their skit.

THINKING BACK AND LOOKING AHEAD

* Are you happy with how your story/skit turned out?
* How did you connect your adjective to the career?
* If there were multiple players, how did you work together?
* How did you share ideas? How were your ideas received by the other players?

COOPERATIVE BALLOON TOWER

In this STEM-based problem-solving activity, kids will build a balloon tower that stands on its own using only the supplies provided. To build problem-solving skills, encourage kids to try multiple strategies, notice what small changes they can make after mistakes, and think outside the box.

Age Range:	5+
Skills:	Problem-solving, cooperation, communication
Materials:	10 inflated balloons, painter's tape, timer (optional)
Number of Participants:	2–3
Where to Play:	Inside or outside

BEFORE YOU START

★ Talk about how players might work together for this task.
★ Review how to share your ideas, offer feedback, and disagree politely. For example, instead of saying this:
  • I have an idea! Let's do it this way.
  • That makes no sense! I have a better idea!
★ Try this:
  • I thought of something! Let's try this....
  • Hmm, I'm not sure if that will work because we tried that over there. Maybe if we do it this way....
  • Okay, that makes sense. Let's try it!

HOW TO PLAY

★ Give players the activity materials. Players will use only these materials to try to build a balloon tower that stands on its own. The balloons should be stacked on top of one another to resemble a skyscraper. Kids can decide if they want a tall, thin tower or if they want a tower with a wider base made up of two or three balloons. It's up to them!
★ You may choose to set a timer to add a layer of difficulty.

THINKING BACK AND LOOKING AHEAD

★ What strategies did you try that didn't work? How did you handle it when things didn't work?
★ How did it feel to keep trying after something didn't work?
★ Why do you think it's important to be persistent, or not give up?
★ How did you work together to accomplish this task?
★ What words or feedback were used that helped you communicate clearly and kindly?

FIND THE LEADER

Attention to detail is the name of the game in this activity. Kids will have to tune in to the body movements of others to find out who is starting a chain of events in the group. Practicing attention to detail and focus will help hone problem-solving skills.

Age Range:	5+
Skills:	Problem-solving, attention to detail
Materials:	None
Number of Participants:	4+
Where to Play:	Inside or outside

BEFORE YOU START
★ Review the rules in depth, as this game can be tricky!
★ Offer some examples of small movements players could use during the game.
★ Talk about how the other players will watch the leader without making it obvious who they are looking at, as this will give away the answer to the guesser.

HOW TO PLAY
★ One player (the guesser) will leave the room. The remaining players pick a leader, or the adult can assign one. Players will spread out and make a circle.
★ When the guesser returns to the room, the leader will begin making small movements that the other players will copy. They should not make any sounds. Players should try to watch the leader without making it too obvious that they are doing so. Examples of small movements could be:
  • Scratching a knee
  • Tapping a finger on a hip
  • Tapping a toe on the floor
★ When the guesser has figured out who the leader is, they can guess.
★ The person who was the leader will then become the guesser for the next round. Play until every child has had the chance to be the leader and the guesser.

THINKING BACK AND LOOKING AHEAD
★ What strategies did you use to watch the leader without giving it away?
★ When you were the guesser, what strategies did you use to figure out who the leader was?
★ Can you think of a situation or place when you could use this skill away from home?

FLIP IT

In this game, children will work together to flip a blanket, sheet, or towel they are standing on without stepping off it. Kids will need to share ideas, strategize, learn from mistakes, and work together to accomplish the task.

Age Range:	5+
Skills:	Problem-solving, cooperation, communication
Materials:	Blanket, sheet, towel, or tarp
Number of Participants:	4+
Where to Play:	Inside or outside

BEFORE YOU START
* Let players share some ideas about how they might complete the task.
* Talk about what they can do if they feel frustrated during the activity: take deep breaths, encourage one another, or try new strategies.

HOW TO PLAY
* Place the blanket (or sheet, towel, or tarp) on the ground. All players will stand on it.
* The goal of the activity is for the players to flip the blanket over completely without anyone stepping off it.
* If a player steps off the blanket, reset it to the starting point.

THINKING BACK AND LOOKING AHEAD
* What was hard about this activity?
* How did you work together?
* How did you handle frustration with the task?
* What strategies did you use to help yourselves work together?
* What would you do differently next time?

STORY SWITCH UP

In this storytelling activity, kids will tell a story but will have to change a key detail when the adult leader calls, "Switch!" Kids will have to use flexible-thinking strategies to change the story and engage in active listening to pick up the story where it was left off.

Age Range:	6+
Skills:	Flexible thinking, active listening
Materials:	None
Number of Participants:	1+
Where to Play:	Inside, outside, or on video chat

BEFORE YOU START
★ Talk about ways you can actively listen to others. For example, you might push other thoughts away, look at their face, listen to their words, and think about what they're saying. Remind kids to pay close attention so they can jump in and change the story details when needed.

HOW TO PLAY
★ Players will sit in a circle. One player will begin telling a story.
★ At any point, the adult leader can call, "Switch!" When the leader says, "Switch!" the next player will continue the story, but they must change what the previous player just said. For example:
  • Player 1: Once upon a time, there was a dragon who was very hungry.
  • Adult: Switch!
  • Player 2: The dragon had just eaten a big dinner, so he wasn't hungry at all. He was on his way to his friend's house to play baseball.
  • Adult: Switch!
  • Player 3: The dragon was on his way to the doctor's office for a checkup.
★ If there is only one player, that's okay—they can switch up their own story.
★ Continue this until the story is complete!

THINKING BACK AND LOOKING AHEAD
★ Was it tricky to switch the story?
★ What strategies did you use to help yourself pay close attention so you could add to the story?

CHAPTER 11

YOU MATTER TOO! RESPECT SKILLS

WHAT IS RESPECT?

Respect is the act of valuing others and treating others as if they are worthy of love and care. It is also a feeling that someone admires your skills, qualities, abilities, or efforts. The experience of respect is both a feeling and an action, as it can be experienced and also shown through behaviors.

WHAT DOES RESPECT LOOK AND SOUND LIKE?

The outward demonstration of respect involves showing others that they matter and are important. This can be done by expressing it verbally or showing it with your actions. Some examples of outward demonstrations of respect include:

★ Letting others know you value or admire their efforts, skills, or achievements
★ Making sure everyone feels safe and welcome
★ Accepting others no matter their differences
★ Listening while others speak
★ Honoring other people's boundaries

RESPECT IN KID-FRIENDLY TERMS

To explain respect to your kid, you could say something like this:

There are so many people in the world! Everyone is unique and different, but we also have a lot in common. Each person has strengths and unique qualities that make them who they are. Respect means that we show and tell people that their ideas, experiences, and qualities are important to us. We can do this by listening while others are talking, including others, and making sure other people feel safe and welcome when they are around us.

WHY RESPECT SKILLS ARE IMPORTANT

Simply stated, respect creates feelings of trust, safety, and connection. When we feel respected, we feel safe to be ourselves and share our ideas. When we show respect to others, they trust us with their ideas and experiences. In environments that include mutual respect, people feel safe to take risks, share ideas, try new things, and be creative. Respect creates an environment where ideas and creativity flow, because people feel safe to be who they are and honor where they came from.

WHERE AND WHEN KIDS WILL USE RESPECT SKILLS

Kids can begin to demonstrate respect in the home environment by being respectful of personal belongings and siblings' boundaries. As they get older, they can show respect in the community by choosing respectful behaviors in grocery stores or picking up their trash after a picnic. As they join activities with more kids from outside their small circle, they'll have the chance to show respect as they learn about peers' experiences, backgrounds, and beliefs. As they enter the school setting, opportunities for respecting school property, teachers, and peers will be around every corner!

LOOKING AHEAD

In this chapter, you'll find games that encourage kids to recognize personal space boundaries of others and consider appropriate actions in a variety of settings. You'll also find opportunities for kids to express respect to others in creative ways and activities that emphasize respectful communication.

RED LIGHT, GREEN LIGHT

Honoring someone's personal space is a great way to be respectful. In this game, kids will get a visual representation of others' personal space preferences.

Age Range:	3+
Skills:	Respect, self-control, active listening
Materials:	None
Number of Participants:	3+
Where to Play:	Outside

BEFORE YOU START

★ Talk about what personal space is. Personal space is the area in which we feel safe in our bodies and we don't want others to enter this space. When others cross into our personal space, we might feel uncomfortable or unsafe.

HOW TO PLAY

★ One player will be the traffic director. The other players will be the drivers. Drivers will stand 20–30 feet away from the traffic director.
★ When the traffic director says, "Green light!" drivers will begin walking toward the traffic director.
★ When the traffic director says, "Yellow light!" drivers will begin to slow down.
★ When the nearest driver is approaching the traffic director's personal space boundary (the area in which they would not like others to enter), the traffic director will say, "Red light!" All drivers will stop moving.
★ When the drivers stop, encourage all players to notice where the traffic director's personal space boundary is.
★ Switch traffic directors and continue playing until everyone has had a chance to be the traffic director.

(continued on next page)

THINKING BACK AND LOOKING AHEAD

★ What did you notice during this activity?

★ Did everyone have the same personal space boundaries?

★ Why is it important to notice where other people's personal space boundaries are?

★ How can we respect someone's personal space?

Personal space is just that—personal! Not all people share the same comfort level about their personal space boundaries. Culture can impact one's personal space preferences as well. This activity will help kids start to understand that, but you can keep practicing out in the community. Notice aloud (quietly) when someone takes a step forward in line, creating more space between them and someone. "I noticed that man stepped forward a little bit. It looks like he wants a little more personal space." For a children's book on personal space, check out *Personal Space Camp* by Julia Cook.

FAMILY PUZZLE

This activity encourages each family member to decorate a puzzle piece to represent themselves, their interests, and their passions. When the puzzle is put together, it will be a blend of the whole family's unique qualities and traits. To promote family respect, talk about how even though we have different interests and personalities, we fit together perfectly.

Age Range:	3+
Skills:	Respect
Materials:	Paper or poster board, art supplies
Number of Participants:	The whole family
Where to Play:	Inside

BEFORE YOU START
★ Help younger children identify symbols they could draw to represent their interests (like a soccer ball, ballet slipper, or paw print) or qualities (a hand for a great helper or a heart for kindness).

HOW TO PLAY
★ Cut a piece of paper (or large poster board depending on how big you'd like the final product to be) into puzzle pieces. There should be one piece per family member.
★ Each family member will decorate their puzzle piece to represent themselves. They can include symbols to represent their interests and skills or simply decorate the piece using designs that they like.
★ When everyone is finished, put the puzzle together. If you used paper, you can glue it on a slightly larger piece of construction paper. If you used a poster board, you can tape it from behind or mount it on larger butcher paper.
★ Let everyone share why they decorated their piece in this way.

THINKING BACK AND LOOKING AHEAD
★ What do you notice as you look at our family puzzle?
★ Are any of the pieces exactly the same?
★ Do any of the pieces have anything in common?
★ How does being a little bit different make our family special?
★ How can we show one another respect even though we are different?

RESPECT BINGO

Turn an errand outing or shopping trip into an opportunity to practice respectful behaviors. Make a bingo card with respectful behaviors and challenge your child to get bingo on their card before you return home. There's nothing better than real-life practice!

Age Range:	4+
Skills:	Respect
Materials:	Paper, pencils
Number of Participants:	1+
Where to Play:	In the community

BEFORE YOU START

★ Decide what elements you and your players want on your bingo card.

HOW TO PLAY

★ With your child, create a bingo card that includes respectful actions or behaviors that your child can do on an outing. Here's an example:

Respect Bingo		
Hold the door open for someone.	Stand back while someone is looking at the shelf (give them personal space).	Wait patiently in line.
Respond to questions from the cashier.	Say "Thank you" when someone helps me.	Wait to speak until Dad is finished talking with the clerk.
Use an appropriate voice level in the store.	Do not touch store displays.	Follow my parents' directions right away.

* While you are out running errands or on a shopping trip, challenge your child to complete the respectful behaviors on the card to cross off all items in a row up, down, or diagonally.
* Each time your child completes one of the behaviors, mark the space on their bingo card.
* If they get a bingo, have a celebration! This could be something intangible like a dance party at home, their favorite playlist in the car ride, or time playing their favorite board game.

THINKING BACK AND LOOKING AHEAD

* Which of these respectful behaviors were easier to do?
* Which were harder?
* What other respectful behaviors do you think you could do next time we go out?
* How did it feel to be respectful?
* How did people respond to you when you were respectful?

COMPLIMENT CIRCLE

Telling people what we like and appreciate about them is a great way to show respect. In this activity, kids will take turns offering genuine compliments and praise to one another.

Age Range:	4+
Skills:	Respect, communication, engagement
Materials:	None
Number of Participants:	3+
Where to Play:	Inside, outside, or on video chat

BEFORE YOU START

★ Talk about what a compliment is and how to make it genuine. A compliment is something that we say to someone to let them know we like their work or their efforts. Genuine compliments are true and are generally about something other than someone's appearance.

★ Here are some examples:
  • I like the details you added to your drawing of that cat.
  • I like how you always include me in games.
  • I like how you didn't give up when you were learning to do a cartwheel.

HOW TO PLAY

★ Participants will sit in a circle.
★ One child will offer a genuine compliment about someone else in the circle.
★ The person who just received a compliment will then offer a genuine compliment to someone else.
★ Continue for several rounds until each child has received at least two genuine compliments.

THINKING BACK AND LOOKING AHEAD

★ How did it feel to get a compliment?
★ How did it feel to give a compliment?
★ Why do you think it's important to notice things that other people are good at doing?

FINDING RESPECT ON THE SCREEN

There's always room for a learning opportunity, even during screen time! While your child is watching a TV show or movie, challenge them to look for examples of respect. Simply asking them to think about and notice respectful behaviors will encourage them to transfer this to their own behavior.

Age Range:	4+
Skills:	Respect
Materials:	Paper and pencil (optional)
Number of Participants:	1+
Where to Play:	Inside

BEFORE YOU START

★ Talk about what respect might look like in the show or movie. It could be one character waiting until another is finished speaking to start talking themselves. It could be a character asking another about their culture's traditions or holidays. Or it could be something simple like a character holding a door open for another.

HOW TO PLAY

★ As you watch a TV show or movie with your child, encourage them to look for examples of respect. Older children can write what they notice on paper if you want.

★ You may choose to pause the show or movie to talk about it in real time or simply have a conversation when it's over about what they noticed.

THINKING BACK AND LOOKING AHEAD

★ What respectful actions or behaviors did you notice?
★ Which of these have you done before?
★ Which of these could you do in the future?
★ How did other characters respond when someone was respectful?
★ How do you think they felt when someone treated them with respect?

(continued on next page)

Looking for some great movies to watch with signs of respect? Try these:

- *Finding Nemo*: Talk about respecting individual differences! Nemo has a smaller fin and others ask questions about it and show acceptance.

- *Zootopia*: Judy Hopps finds new ways to contribute to her community in her job even though a bunny has never done that job before. She also respects the community and wants to uphold the laws. Talk about respecting what everyone contributes to the community and respecting the community and rules (and for older children, you can talk about how sometimes the rules or laws do not show respect to individuals).

- *Babe*: Babe learns how to earn respect by showing respect to his fellow farm animals. Talk about how showing respect to others encourages them to show respect too.

RESPECT DETECTIVES

Sometimes errands can be draining for kids, so use a game like this to keep them engaged and motivated while you're out and about. Kids will look for clues and signs of respect in the community. This activity will also encourage kids to think about ways they can respect their community and be good community members.

Age Range:	4+
Skills:	Respect
Materials:	Paper and pencils (optional)
Number of Participants:	1+
Where to Play:	In the community

BEFORE YOU START
★ Talk about what you might look for. Signs of disrespect are easier to identify: litter, unwanted graffiti, or rogue shopping carts. Signs of respect may be harder to identify but could include noticing people throwing their trash away or picking things up that they dropped, seeing someone stay on the sidewalk instead of walking through plants, or seeing people return their shopping carts instead of letting them roll away in the parking lot.

HOW TO PLAY
★ Go for a drive or a walk in the community.
★ With your child, look for signs of respect or disrespect in the community. Talk about what you notice!
★ When you get home, brainstorm a list of ways kids can show respect to their community or, if appropriate, address some of the signs of disrespect that they noticed (e.g., do a trash-pick-up day in the park).

THINKING BACK AND LOOKING AHEAD
★ What signs of respect did you notice? Are these things you already do? Could do?
★ Did this give you any ideas for other ways that you could show respect to your community?
★ What do you think you could do to address any of the signs of disrespect that you saw in the community?

GOLDEN RULE

Treat others how you'd like to be treated: The Golden Rule is a great guiding principle for being respectful, but it's important to know what that means for you personally. This game encourages kids to spend some time self-reflecting via creative writing so they know exactly how they'd like to be treated and what it would look like to treat others this way.

Age Range:	5+
Skills:	Respect, empathy
Materials:	Paper, pencil, coloring utensils (optional)
Number of Participants:	1+
Where to Play:	Inside

BEFORE YOU START
★ Make a list of how your child would like to be treated. You can guide this discussion with questions like:
  • How would you like for other people to talk to you?
  • What would you like for other people to do when they notice you are sad?
  • How would you like for other people to treat you on the playground?

HOW TO PLAY
★ Be sure you have written down how your child wants to be treated by others.
★ Then, challenge your child to write a story about how they could treat someone this way. Encourage them to be creative in their story and include lots of details.
★ Your child can illustrate the story if they'd like to as well.

THINKING BACK AND LOOKING AHEAD
★ How easy do you think it will be for you to treat others how you want to be treated?
★ How do you think you could help yourself remember to treat other people this way?

COMPLIMENT POETRY

Giving genuine compliments and noticing people's strengths are great ways to show that you care about them and respect them and their efforts! In this activity, kids will take time to creatively express respect for others by writing a poem about them.

Age Range:	5+
Skills:	Respect, engagement
Materials:	Paper, pencils
Number of Participants:	2+
Where to Play:	Inside

BEFORE YOU START

★ Talk about what a genuine compliment is: Genuine compliments are true things we say to or about people to share positive things we notice and like about them. They are generally about something other than someone's appearance.

HOW TO PLAY

★ Each child will write a poem about another person.
★ Give kids time to think about someone else's strengths, skills, or efforts. What do they do well? What did they try really hard on?
★ Kids will then write a poem to offer compliments to this person about their strengths, skills, or efforts. Here are a couple of examples:

Example 1: Rhyming Poem	Example 2: Acrostic Poem
Max always has a smile Painted across his face. He makes everyone feel welcome Like they're in the right place!	M—makes everyone feel special R—really good at math S.—smiles at everyone in the morning J—joyful all the time O—one great teacher N—never laughs at mistakes E—easy to talk to S—silly joke teller

THINKING BACK AND LOOKING AHEAD

★ How do you think this person will feel when they read or hear your poem?
★ Why do you think it's important to notice positive things about people?

CALL ETIQUETTE

Landline phones may be a thing of the past, but telephone or video-conference etiquette is not. In this activity, kids will practice respectful ways of talking on the phone or on video calls.

Age Range:	5+
Skills:	Respect, communication
Materials:	Play phone, real phone, or video chat device
Number of Participants:	1+
Where to Play:	Inside or on video chat

BEFORE YOU START

★ Review the following teaching points. Discuss appropriate voice volume as well.
★ Practice making a call. For example, use a greeting and identify yourself.
  • Example: Hello, this is Genevieve Parker.
  • Example: Good morning! This is James.
★ Tell them why you are calling or ask to speak to the person you'd like to talk to.
  • Example: May I please speak to Grandma?
  • Example: I am calling to invite you to dinner on Friday.
★ Enjoy your conversation! Tell the person what you called to tell them or ask questions and listen to their responses.
  • Example: How is your day going?
  • Example: I wanted to tell you that I came in second place in the science fair!
★ Practice etiquette for ending a call by letting the person know you enjoyed talking with them.
  • Example: Grandma, it was really nice to talk to you today.
  • Example: Mr. Smith, I'm glad I got to talk to you.
★ Let the person know you need to go.
  • Example: I need to go finish my homework.
  • Example: It's time for me to set the table.
★ End with a goodbye statement.
  • Example: Goodbye!
  • Example: See you on Friday. Bye!

* Now practice answering the phone. First, say hello and identify yourself.
  * Example: Hello, this is Marcus.
  * Example: Good morning, this is Kyrie in Mrs. Jacob's class.
* Gather information. Listen for the person's name or their request. Remember or write down the person's name and what they ask for or why they are calling.
* Give information. Let them know why you are answering or what is going on.
  * Example: My mom is driving right now, but I will give her this message so that she can call you back when we get home.
  * Example: Mrs. Jacob is teaching reading groups right now. Would you like for me to give her a message or ask her to come to the phone?
* Pass along information or end the call.
  * Example: Just a moment. Mom, Nana just wanted to tell you her doctor's appointment is at three o'clock. Okay, I told her, Nana. She'll call you later. Bye!
  * Example: Please wait a moment. I will ask Mrs. Jacob to come to the phone.
* Practice etiquette for video calls:
  * Sit calmly in front of the screen and stay there.
  * If using a phone or a tablet, set the device on a solid surface instead of holding it and moving it during the call.
  * Make eye contact with the person while talking.
  * Keep your focus on the call. Put away toys or other devices.

HOW TO PLAY

* First, practice making a phone call, then ending the phone call at the end of the conversation. Do this with a pretend phone as you practice, then let your child call a family member or friend for real-life practice.
* Next, practice answering a phone call. Older children may be asked to do this when a parent's hands are full or when an adult is driving, or even as a class job when they're at school, so it's a good skill to start practicing early. Again, practice with a pretend phone and then let them have real-life practice.
* Finally, practice taking part in a video call. Sit face-to-face with your child and pretend you're communicating through a screen, or get on two devices in different rooms and do a practice call.
* See the Before You Start section for tips on teaching each of these skills.

THINKING BACK AND LOOKING AHEAD

* How did you feel when you got to make a phone call?
* How did you feel when you got to answer a phone call?
* Why do you think it's important to be respectful when we're using the phone?
* Why do you think it's important to put away toys before we talk on a video call?

IN OR OUT OF BOUNDS

Understanding and respecting personal boundaries is an important social skill in all settings. In this activity, kids will consider certain behaviors or actions and decide if they are okay with them or not (identifying their own personal boundaries) and think about social boundaries as well. Understanding their own boundaries will help kids learn to respect other people's boundaries too.

Age Range:	5+
Skills:	Respect, self-control
Materials:	Hula-Hoops
Number of Participants:	2+
Where to Play:	Inside or outside

BEFORE YOU START

★ Talk about what a boundary is. A boundary is like a fence or a limit. If we are not okay with something, we set a boundary to let others know we are not okay with that. Other people may also set a boundary to let us know that they are not okay with something. Setting a boundary is like building a fence. We are letting others know that we do not want them to cross the boundary. If someone sets a boundary with us, like telling us that they do not want a hug, we can show them respect by not crossing that boundary. In this example, we could ask if they'd like a high five instead of a hug!

★ When thinking about boundaries, it's important to remember that everyone is in charge of their own bodies. Also, boundaries can change, and we need to respect them every time. Even if someone was okay with a hug last time we saw them, they might not be okay with one this time, and that's okay.

HOW TO PLAY

★ Give each player a Hula-Hoop.

★ Read the following statements (or create your own list). If players are okay with the actions being done to or near them, they will hop in the Hula-Hoop. If they are not okay with the action, they will hop out of the Hula-Hoop. For social-boundary statements, kids will hop in the Hula-Hoop if the behavior is okay in a social setting and hop out of the Hula-Hoop if it's not okay in a social setting.

Personal Boundaries	Social Boundaries
A friend giving me a hug	Running in the grocery store
A family member giving me a hug	Coloring in a coloring book while in a restaurant
Someone I haven't met before giving me a hug	Listening to music with headphones while on a subway or bus
A family member standing close to me while talking	Listening to music without headphones while on a subway or bus
A friend standing close to me while talking	Talking on the phone in a restaurant
Someone I haven't met before standing close to me while talking	Watching a movie on the iPad during church/synagogue/mosque
Someone asking to play a game with me	Talking to the person in line behind you at the grocery store
Someone watching me play a game	Touching the things in the cart of the person behind you in line at the grocery store
Someone joining me in a game without asking	High-fiving or shaking hands with the other team after your team loses a game
A sibling coming into my room without knocking	Ignoring the other team after your team loses a game
A family member tickling me	Booing at your sibling's soccer game
A friend tickling me	Reading a book at your sibling's game
A family member touching things that are special to me	Touching someone's food on their plate without asking
A friend touching things that are special to me	Asking if you can try a family member's food
Someone I don't know touching things that are special to me	Knocking before you go into someone's house or room
A family member touching me while they talk to me	Walking into a friend's house without knocking on the door
A friend touching me while they talk to me	Wearing a sibling's clothes without asking

(continued on next page)

THINKING BACK AND LOOKING AHEAD

★ Which of these things were you not okay with?
★ If playing with more than one child, did you all have the same boundaries? Which ones were different?
★ Why is it important to respect other people's boundaries?
★ Why is it important to tell other people what our boundaries are?
★ Why is it important to think about boundaries in places in the community like restaurants, stores, and subways?
★ How can we show others respect when they set boundaries?
★ How can we respect people in the community by respecting boundaries?

RECIPE FOR RESPECT

In this silly, creative activity, kids will think about what "ingredients" go into showing respect to others and the community. They'll create their own "recipe for respect" as a reminder for what they can do.

Age Range:	5+
Skills:	Respect
Materials:	Paper, pencils, coloring utensils
Number of Participants:	1+
Where to Play:	Inside

BEFORE YOU START

★ Look at a cookbook together to see how recipes are written.
★ Make a list about what your child thinks is important in showing respect. Brainstorm symbols to represent each portion of the recipe so they can include these in their drawing if they want to.

HOW TO PLAY

★ Talk with your child about what goes into showing respect. Is it listening? Is it caring? Is it kindness? Which of these are most important?
★ Let your child create their own "recipe for respect." They can write their ingredients list and draw a picture that represents respect. Here's an example of what an ingredient list might look like:

My Recipe for Respect
- A dash of listening
- A pinch of understanding
- A bit of caring
- A heavy pour of kindness

THINKING BACK AND LOOKING AHEAD

★ What ingredients did you include? Why did you choose these?
★ Which ones do you think are most important?
★ Which ingredient is hardest for you to include in real life? How can I help you with this?

3

PRACTICAL APPLICATION

The activities and games included in Part 2 of this book are fun, interactive ways to practice these important social skills, but there is room for growth outside of games too! In Part 3, we will discuss meaningful and practical ways that you can weave social-skill development into your everyday life and conversations to encourage kids to better understand themselves and the world around them.

Some of these methods of practicing social skills at home will take time and consistent practice to make positive changes. Ongoing practice will give kids the best opportunity for growth and learning that they'll retain. Investing the time in the "long game" will pay off as kids feel comfortable to practice skills in the safety of their family unit.

CHAPTER 12

INCORPORATING SKILLS INTO EVERYDAY LIFE

DAILY WAYS TO APPLY SOCIAL SKILLS

The foundational building blocks of social skills are seeing, thinking, and acting. Younger children jump straight to acting, being led by impulses. As they get older, they are better able to take in information by observing the world around them. And as they get older still and develop maturity, kids are able to take in information through observation, then pause to think about and interpret this information in order to make an informed decision about appropriate actions. This process takes time and will, of course, have room for error as kids try skills and actions, receive feedback from others, and learn about how their behaviors are received by the people and the world around them. Finding ways every day to reinforce these skills will help kids master them faster and more completely.

Communication Skills

Our daily lives are full of opportunities for practicing communication skills using verbal and nonverbal communication. To be intentional about building these skills, try the following strategies:

* **Make time for meaningful conversations:** Life gets busy! Sometimes intentional conversations fall by the wayside in the busyness of life. Set aside time each day to have focused, intentional conversations with kids. Sit together in your favorite spot without devices or distractions and just talk for 5–10 minutes. Ask your child questions like:
  * What were you proud of today?
  * What was confusing today?
  * What made you laugh today?
  * What questions do you have for me?
* **Model effective communication:** Adults aren't perfect, and that's okay. But making an effort to model effective communication skills will go a long way in setting an example for kids. Be mindful of these communication strategies:
  * Clearly share how you feel. Use "I" statements, like, "I feel frustrated when I can't find my car keys. I need a few minutes to myself to focus on finding

them." Or "I feel excited because we're going camping this weekend! It'll be nice to have some time away from our busy routine."

- Be mindful of tone of voice and voice volume.
- Be mindful of your own body language and nonverbal communication. Does it match your words? Kids take cues from us in learning how to use their own nonverbal communication skills.

★ **Provide gentle guidance:** When your child isn't communicating effectively or when they use inappropriate voice volume or tone of voice, get down on their level, make eye contact, and provide gentle guidance, like, "Hey, buddy, we're inside, but your voice level is really high, like you might use at a baseball game. Let's try again with a lower voice volume."

★ **Apply learning in everyday life:** If you've been practicing voice volume, put it to practice in real life! Head out for a trip to the library, the park, and the grocery store. Encourage your child to think about what voice volume is appropriate in each setting.

Active-Listening Skills

While you practice communication skills, active listening comes alongside as a companion skill. While you are communicating with kids, you can demonstrate active listening while they speak to serve as a model. These strategies will provide opportunities for active listening:

★ **Make time for meaningful conversations:** Again, carving out time for distraction-free conversation sets up kids and adults alike with time to practice actively listening while others share about their days, interests, or concerns.

★ **Provide gentle guidance:** When you notice that your child isn't listening to others, provide gentle guidance, like, "I noticed when your sister was telling you about her day, you were flipping through your book and turning your back to her. How can you show her that you are listening and that you care about her?"

Cooperation Skills

Cooperation doesn't have to be limited to team games! Many household activities can be cooperative activities as well. Sometimes, tasks are easier to complete on our own, but letting kids join in for cooperative practice will go a long way. Try making these activities cooperative in your everyday life:

★ **Laundry:** One person sorts by person, one person folds, one person puts away.
★ **Cooking:** Find a role for everyone in making lunch or dinner.
★ **Grocery shopping:** If two caregivers can go, kids split up with caregivers to tackle the shopping list and shop in half the time.

Responsibility Skills

Many of the responsibility activities in this book are focused on home responsibilities that are already a part of your everyday life. To expand on this and encourage kids to think meaningfully about responsibility, make time for meaningful discussions around the topic. Talk about things like:

* How does this responsibility contribute to our family?
* How would our family be affected if you didn't do this responsibility?
* How do you feel about being able to contribute to our family in this way?
* What was it like to take responsibility for this task/behavior/action?

Empathy Skills

Empathy is a skill that relies upon other social skills. To truly be empathetic, kids need to be able to communicate effectively, pick up on body language and facial expressions, and be great at active listening. When kids are empathetic, engagement comes more easily, and they are more respectful of others' feelings, belongings, and boundaries. To promote empathy skills in your everyday life, try these strategies:

* **Make time for talking about feelings:** To understand feelings, kids need to have an emotional vocabulary. They need to have words to describe their feelings. They need to hear others talk about feelings so they can understand how others experience things. Set aside time each day for family members to talk about how they are feeling and why they feel that way. This is a great opportunity to practice communication, active listening, and empathy skills together.

* **Model empathy:** When your child has strong emotions, model empathetic responses. This can simply sound like reflecting their feelings back to them, like, "You felt sad when they didn't include you in the game." Or you can demonstrate an empathetic response, like, "You felt disappointed when you weren't picked for the team. When I feel disappointed, I like to have a hug. Would you like to have a hug or is there another way I can support you?" Modeling empathy consistently at home will help kids see what it looks like so they can replicate it in social settings.

* **Provide gentle guidance:** When your child responds to siblings or family members in ways that are not empathetic, provide gentle reminders of ways they can show empathy instead. For example, "When your sister was crying after she got hurt, you rolled your eyes and walked past her. How do you think you might feel if someone did that when you were hurt? Can you think of a way to show empathy to your sister instead? What could you say or do to show her that you care about how she feels?"

* **Apply learning in everyday life:** As you are out and about in your community, guide conversations about what you see. Notice a person in the parking lot who is struggling with their shopping cart. "It looks like she's having a hard time with

that. I could help her put that shopping cart away to show her I care." Or "That man is living on the sidewalk. I wonder what it's like to walk in his shoes." Noticing these things aloud will not only model empathy for your kids but encourage them to think about what they see in the community as well.

Engagement Skills

Opportunities for engaging with others are all around in everyday life. While games finding common interests are fun, you can encourage kids to engage with others in the neighborhood, in the community, at school, and beyond as you go about your normal life. To encourage kids to engage with others, try these strategies:

★ Invite friends over for playdates or meet up at a local park.
★ When you go to a park, encourage your child to play with someone they don't know yet and get to know them.
★ When you run errands, encourage your child to engage with people who engage with them (to whatever degree you are comfortable). They can respond to questions from cashiers, say hello to other shoppers, or notice things they have in common with people they see in stores.
★ Sign up for activities and events. There's no need to overextend yourself or your child, but sign up for an activity your child enjoys so that they have the chance to engage with peers outside of the family unit or their typical social group.
★ Model engagement for your child. When you're out, engage with others in stores and be responsive to those who engage with you. This shows kids that engaging with others is important and meaningful and will help them develop a sense of acceptable social boundaries and safety.

Self-Control Skills

Self-control is one of those skills that takes time to develop, but it's an important social skill for kids to cultivate in order to meaningfully interact with peers and engage in the community. Being able to control their bodies and words will go a long way in helping them form and maintain friendships and be great team members. Try these strategies for practicing self-control in your everyday activities:

★ **Implement wait times:** Self-control is all about inhibiting impulses and remaining in control of body and words. When kids want something, try implementing a wait time. This could look like, "I hear that you want to watch TV. Our toys are still out from this morning, so let's set a timer for ten minutes. We'll clean as much as we can in those ten minutes, and then we will watch TV." This helps kids see the importance of waiting and fulfilling a responsibility before getting a desired activity or thing.
★ **Model self-control:** Seeing caregivers practice self-control will help kids understand the importance of practicing it themselves. This can simply look

like talking aloud about how you are inhibiting your impulses. For example, "I really want to watch my favorite TV show, but I have some work I need to finish. I'll finish this task and then I'll watch my favorite show after that." Hearing a caregiver explain the rationale for implementing self-control will help kids make a connection between responsibilities and self-control.

★ **Provide gentle guidance:** When your child is not using self-control, particularly in a public place, get down on their level, make eye contact, and provide gentle guidance. "It seems like you're having a hard time controlling your body while we are in this store. I am noticing that you are touching a lot of things on the shelves, but we have talked about how we should not do that while we are in stores. Let's take a moment and breathe together to calm our bodies. Then, we can try to keep shopping using our self-control." Or you can use this as an opportunity to make connections to others. "I noticed when you climbed to the top of the play structure, you jumped in front of the line for the slide. Those children were waiting, and it looked like they were upset and frustrated when you did not wait for your turn. This is a chance to practice your self-control! Self-control can look like waiting for your turn in the line. Would you like to try again so that you can help your friends feel safe and happy while they play too?"

★ **Apply learning in everyday life:** As you go about your day, simply point out or talk about ways your child can demonstrate self-control. For example, "We're going to the library today. Remember, in the library we can use self-control by being in control of our voice level."

Emotion-Regulation Skills

Emotion regulation in real life looks like noticing, honoring, and dealing with emotions as they come. All feelings are okay to have, but sometimes we need a strategy to help us feel better and cope. To promote emotion regulation in everyday life, employ these strategies:

★ **Label emotions:** When kids have big feelings, help them label the feelings and recognize that the physical and emotional experiences have names.

★ **Honor the feeling:** Be responsive to kids' feelings. This can simply be restating the feeling, or it can be validating the feeling, such as, "You're feeling angry because you feel like things aren't fair."

★ **Help your child regulate feelings:** Kids need guidance as they learn to regulate their emotions. Sending kids to their rooms to regulate on their own will only send the message that their feelings aren't acceptable and should be dealt with in private. Kids may feel the need to hide their feelings when this is the norm. Together, practice calming strategies to show kids that their feelings are acceptable to you and that you want to help them learn to manage them. As you practice together over time, kids will find strategies that work for them and be confident that they can employ the strategies independently when they have big feelings.

★ **Reflect:** After an emotionally charged event and after kids have regulated their emotions, reflect with them on what happened. What triggered the feeling? What strategy helped your child feel better? What can they do if they face this triggering event again in the future?

Problem-Solving Skills

Everyday life is full of problems to be solved, right? Problem-solving tasks don't have to be elaborate STEM challenges with a lot of materials. Tasks can be as mundane as fitting all the dishes in the dishwasher or rearranging the bookshelf so that it's easier to find favorite books. Encourage kids to engage in problem-solving thinking with these strategies:

★ **Talk through and model your own problem-solving tasks:** This might sound like, "Hmm, I'm trying to load these groceries into the back of the car, and I'm not sure how they will all fit in here. I might need to move this box over here and that bag over here. I'll need to stack these and gently lay these here.... Hmm, it just might fit."

★ **Provide gentle guidance:** When your child faces a problem at home, resist the urge to bail them out! Encourage them to think through the task, try new strategies, learn from any mistakes that they make in the task, think about past experiences and how they can apply to this problem, and avoid the urge to give up. Provide gentle guiding questions, like, "Remember when you solved that other problem? How could you use what you did there to help you here?"

★ **Apply learning in everyday life:** When your child solves a problem, don't let the problem-solving stop there! Encourage them to think of ways they can apply this problem-solving process to other problems. What other situations could you apply this to? What other problems might you be able to solve now that you've solved this one? What else do you want to know about this problem or similar problems?

Respect Skills

Opportunities for respect will come into play every day within the family unit, the neighborhood, and the community. You can also talk about ways to show respect that kids may not even know about!

★ Ways to show respect in everyday life:
  • **In the family:** Talk about and practice respecting family members' personal space, boundaries, ideas, and unique qualities.
  • **In the neighborhood:** Talk about and practice respecting neighbors' property and noise preferences.

- **In the community:** Talk about and practice respecting community rules, community land, and community resources like lakes, parks, wildlife, and community art.
* **Share about how you show respect:** Throughout the day, point out ways that you are being respectful to help kids understand the subtle and not-so-subtle ways they can show respect. This could sound like, "My boss is calling me. I am going to move into a quiet space to talk to her because it would be hard for her to hear me in here, and that's an easy way for me to show her respect." Or "My phone is ringing. I will not answer it while we're in the library because people are trying to read. I'll wait until we get outside to call back. That's an easy way for me to be respectful of the rules of the library and other people's space."

FINAL THOUGHTS

Social skills are important for cohesion in the family unit, developing and maintaining friendships outside of the family, participating in group events like sports or extracurricular clubs, meaningfully contributing in academic settings with peers, and engaging beyond into adulthood and careers. These skills require an understanding of oneself and the ways in which each of us relates to others and the world around us. Meaningful connections formed through the use of positive social skills give kids and adults a sense of belonging and connectedness that directly impacts physical and mental health and future success.

While the importance of social skills is clear, there remain a variety of paths kids can take to practice social skills. Kids develop at different rates and in different ways, and that's okay. Use the activities in this book to enrich your relationships and the ways in which you help your child understand the world and others around them. Each child's path will look a little different, and that's part of what makes kids amazing! Enjoy your time growing together.

INDEX